A MILLION DREAMS

FOR THE WORLD WE'RE GONNA MAKE

INAYAT SINGAL

INDIA · SINGAPORE · MALAYSIA

Notion Press

No.8, 3rd Cross Street,
CIT Colony, Mylapore,
Chennai, Tamil Nadu – 600004

First Published by Notion Press 2021
Copyright © Inayat Singal 2021
All Rights Reserved.

ISBN 978-1-64951-623-7

CONTENTS

ACKNOWLEDGEMENTS

To all the people who have helped me in this endeavor, On this journey of finding myself in sustainability-my teachers, friends and vast extended family, My circle of strong-willed youth, wanting to make a difference, My eternal mentor, Dr. Daisaku Ikeda, who continues to inspire me every moment of life To the loves of my life: Ishani Singal, my sister who has taught me to stand by my ideals, And above all, Ritu Singal, my most loving mother who has taught me courage.

PREFACE

The idea behind this book came when my mom encouraged me to write about my understanding of sustainable development goals. The sustainable development goals are 17 targets made by United Nations towards creating a better world by 2030. The targets include education, health, economy, etc in it's agenda. What I have tried to do through this book is put the goals in a way that is very relevant to our everyday actions. However, the journey has been a long one. I started dreaming about a better world as a kid. I observed through books, movies and people around me that everyone was suffering. I saw children cry of hunger, politicians thinking about personal gain, young people giving up and the picture was not a bed of roses with countless natural calamities on the top of it all. The song 'Heal the World' by Micheal Jackson and the composition 'Ode to Joy' by Beethoven however always had a way with me. These gave me the courage to believe in a better world that would be created by me and by people like me.

I got to study about sustainable development goals given by UN, first in 2015 and remember looking at these goals as the way into a new age. I read the 17 goals and knew the journey would be long and definitely not easy. But like it is said "The fire inside me burned brighter than the fire around me." I wanted to talk to the youth about the goals and shout out to anyone who wanted to be a part of a better world, let's do it.

I went about telling people only to realize half of the youth didn't know about these goals and the other half felt they couldn't do anything about it and had already given up. There was another segment of them too busy in their own lives to bother. However, when I read lives of great men and women of the past I learnt that optimism combined with action was the only way out.

As I walked towards the dawn of a new age as a youth, I observed. I observed the millennials read about the work done by organisations like the UN or read about the policies taken by the government and feel indifferent. In 2015 when sustainable development goals came people were questioning "What can I do?" I observed youth put everything on the shoulders of the government while the world kept hoping that youth would change the world.

I meanwhile was focused on what could be done rather than what couldn't. The world has seen setbacks. It has been let down by people in power on various occasions, it, but what if change makers like Nelson Mandela or Rosa Parks were busy criticizing what was wrong without taking action. Would the world have progressed towards what was right.

When Megallan took the sails and slowly not in giant leaps but small steps covered the planet, he realised it was round. Similarly, when we start walking on this path to change the world, we realise the change lies not in one person taking a thousand steps, it is in thousand people taking one step as said by Dr. Daisaku Ikeda. Transformation lies in changing our heart. By creating heart to care for those who are vulnerable and by converting that care into action, in our own unique ways, we can change the world.

In a world where youth is living in the shackles of powerlessness and apathy this book was written to create awareness by suggesting ways to create a sustainable way of living, rooted in the understanding of respect for dignity of life.

It started with me wondering what a perfect world would look like. First I thought a world without wars seemed a good place to live in and then this pandemic happened. I thought these diseases too must be eliminated. Gradually as I began understanding things in a better light I realised that every problem in this world stems from disrespect towards life, be it others life or our own. Wars happen when we don't see other people as good enough, health hazards when we don't respect our bodies. Hence to me, a perfect world will be one with respect for life.

So today, I present this book to every youth in the world telling: you can make a difference. You can make a difference wherever you are, whoever you are. Its only about making a determination to respect life. I know that you get bored with lengthy lectures and I'm not here to give you another one. I am writing this with anecdotes from my own life, my friends' lives and my family's experiences that if you believe you can do it, you can.

Through my own journey as a school going child and further as a college student, I have tried to present to the youth what we can do to make the sustainable development goals a reality. I am a student like any other, without any association with big organisations but what I do have is a big heart with big dreams. This journey is surely not easy but through this book I have tried to introduce 17 sustainable development goals in a way that is relatable so that someday everyone who is reading this can create their own book to create a sustainable future.

I'll end this preface with poetic words of Mr. Krishna Srinivas

".....Galactic clouds

Of interstellar dust

Measuring light years

And millions of suns.....

From the phoenix of realities

Will suddenly bloom a new Eden-

A Race of stalwart men

And flower women

With eyes to see

Histories in make and ears to hear

Luring music from far off space."

So, let's journey together, on this road of constructing a new age, a new beginning, the youthful world citizens together.

FOREWORD

Dr. Shruti Shukla

The problems we are facing today transcend national and social boundaries. The SDGs should not only be seen as policy guidelines for governments but also alarm bells for citizens to change their way of life. This book sensitizes, motivates and nudges all of us to act against world problems like poverty, health, quality education, climate change, malnutrition, gender equality, Issues related with natural resources, biodiversity, sanitization, etc.. This book effectively explains the need for collective action and suggests a grassroots action plan to tackle the same. Think globally and act locally is reflected in all SDGs and nicely interpreted by the young author.

Author has laid an emphasis on capabilities of youth and also suggested ...how can a youth help in attaining these goals in a very practical manner. Every individual can make a difference, and this thought motivated the author so much and she motivated further all and one towards achieving quality of life.

Inayat strongly believed indignity of life, and that is the crux of life also. It is only possible through compassion and courage .. this is only wisdom that takes everyone towards a sustainable future. Inayat tried to express her views on knowledge and wisdom also. The author made it very clear that understanding these goals will make road map clear to achieve a sustainable future also. Inayat has put all concepts, related to sustainability in a very simple way by giving examples and anecdotes.

This is an interesting read for all those who want to be the change they want to see.

My best wishes to Inayat!

Dr. Shruti Shukla

Educationist, Environmentalist and career Counselor

SCERT

Govt of Punjab

Juan Pablo Ramirez Miranda

"The SDGs are an ambitious agenda to build a peaceful and sustainable world, and youth action is key for them to become a reality. Inayat's personal reflection on how each SDG relates to daily life and each person's journey is a great example of the type of engagement and commitment that is required for their successful achievement."

Juan Pablo Ramirez Miranda

Head of social and human sciences at the UNESCO New Delhi Cluster Office

Johan Galtung

Good things start as visions, like dreams, often as positive visions in dreams. Bad things may start as nightmares. Dream positive, to think and speak positive, to act positive, for peace!

This book will help you.

Johan Galtung

Norwegian sociologist and principal founder of the field of peace and conflict studies

David Krieger

"This is a book that can change the world. It is written with insight, heart, and hope in the determined belief that change is possible. The author, a 21-year-old medical student, seeks nothing less than a world with justice and dignity for all. She is dreaming big and wants her contemporaries to join her in creating this world."

Founder and President Emeritus

Nuclear Age Peace Foundation

RESPECT FOR
DIGNITY OF LIFE

No Poverty

The poverty bestowed
Is lived when endured
The light restored
Is when hope is endowed

"It's a very remarkable circumstance that poverty and oysters always seem to go together."

– Charles Dickens

The term poverty finds its origins in the word pauper. It almost immediately gets our mind running and is something we can readily relate to the slums in almost every city of India, to the homeless in the USA and to the refugees in Europe. It very classically, though a word acts more in numerical capacity because every time we think of it, the value of 1.9 dollars a day pops up in the minds of most of us. It is a word which on hearing grips our hearts with fear and powerlessness. And so indisputably it is almost a phrase which acts in various capacities of language, number and emotions. However, to create a world without poverty it is important to understand what exactly we are trying to eliminate.

Last year, I got an opportunity as a part of a survey conducted by the community medicine department of my college to visit houses in a small village, Kateel in the southern part of India. The survey was conducted to understand the living conditions of people living in the tiny village known for a famous temple. This meant walking long distances in the exhausting June heat. Like every other student dehydrated and pretty irritated with the entire process I was complaining of how drained I was. In between a heated discussion of how useless the activity was my group mates and I ended up on the doorsteps of the next house we were to survey. We saw a lady in her early forties standing at the door almost as if to welcome us.

The five of us however couldn't control the expressions on our face when we looked at her thatched hut which was damaged beyond repair. We could see the water collected on the roof, dripping into the hut. With only 2 bulbs the house seemed to be living in the shackles of the darkest hours of life. We could not help but have sympathy for her.

She was however not bothered by our expressions. She through her friendly yet striking demeanour conveyed that she knew how to stand tall and strong despite the hardships. She shed no tears while telling us how some days the choice was to be made between electricity and the food. However, listening to her and observing the way she stood, my heart did not allow me to feel pity for her even though the logistics said otherwise.

She owned the hardships that is what her body language indicated. On the other hand, my mind quizzed itself at the thought that isn't this what true poverty is. The facts of her narrative did reflect that. To anyone taking note of her living conditions, she was a poor lady with three daughters in a male dominated society, who had lost her husband, the sole bread earner of the family. She was hardly able to sustain her family after his death and was trying to hold on by working as a house help in the few houses in the village, who could afford it. Putting food on the table everyday was a struggle. She said, some days her children would sleep without a single grain of food in their bellies. To me, it didn't seem things could become worse. Looking at her plight the thought of the slums I had seen across the country over the course of my life came to my mind. The children in those slums sobbing with hunger and with hopelessness, their eyes say "This is what destiny has in store for us. This is where we belong."

Taking my mind back to the conversation going on I couldn't help but notice something peculiar about the lady. It was her eyes. They didn't resemble the kids from the slums. Her eyes seemed to tell a different story. It was as if those black eyes with a spark of hope said "I climb the steep mountain, with a heavy backpack climbing the summit while enjoying the view."

On our further questioning we found out that her eldest daughter was studying arts in a college in a nearby city while the two younger ones were going to school and were following the footsteps of the elder sibling. Soon we all understood that this lady was not going to give up in the face of hardships by blaming what destiny had created for her. She was there to show the world how to move on. In that instant I understood what her eyes were saying. Through the hardships of life which were as steep as the mountain, with the backpack of her karma she had decided to win. She had decided to reach the summit, without wasting time to begrudge her life because she was busy enjoying the journey.

That incident taught me something about the first sustainable development goal that poverty is not the absence of money or even food. It's a mindset. It's a state of insecurity that exists externally due to our circumstances but leads to building of internal walls of I/ he/ she can't do this.

In that moment I realised, I was the pauper not her. In that moment I understood, poverty is another word for not appreciating the power of life which the lady however had learnt better. Something that her body language and eyes clearly indicated was yet to be understood by my heart.

At no moment in that half an hour conversation did she ever feel she was different than us because she knew the power of her life. She, like each one of us was born to be happy and she understood that her life had the potential to create that happiness for herself and her family.

As I saw her walk back to her hut, I couldn't help thinking that how she was ready to break the shackles of the darkest hour with the light of hope that burned bright deep in her life.

The activity may have seemed useless to me at that point but it made me understand the importance of asking myself, whether it was me who was locked in chains of poverty through my mindset? I extend this question to all the readers.

Do we tell ourselves or others around us that this is where we belong or do we look at our problems and circumstances in the eye and tell them just watch me climb the summit enjoying the view?

LEARNING POINTS

1. The sustainable development goal of no poverty talks of eradication of poverty in all form which starts from changing our mindset

2. The way forward is by believing in the power and potential of human life.

3. When our mind and heart change, we are able to start a positive feedback loop

4. Action to educate and create awareness is the starting point to creating a world without poverty.

Zero Hunger

The cries, the sighs

The moments that don't seem to pass by

The horror of times that lie

Shall pass by only if kindness shall never die

"If you can't feed a hundred people then feed just one"

– Mother Teresa

Hunger, doesn't this term always seem to be more than a word. The depth in this 5-letter word even exceeds the depth in some sentences or even some poems sometimes. When I come across this word instantly my brain paints a mural of two hands begging for food. And this picture my friends, somehow has the art to provoke me. It elicits almost as a reflex itself, the faces of people split between the will to exist and die at the same time. It is a word that brings the poem 'The Rime of the Ancient Mariner' by Samuel Taylor Coleridge to my mind. Hunger finds a way to mock me, reflecting through the eyes of the mariner, who is living a life conflicted between life in death and death in life. The irony of this poem which is put together in 7 parts by the poet is however, conveyed in this 5-letter word 'hunger', not enough to live or die.

When this word however comes to my mind it is always accompanied with words of Buzz Aldrin "If we can conquer space, we can conquer world hunger,"

Having been fortunate enough to have had comfortable living and apathy being the new definition of cool some years back. I was busy chilling in my comfort zone with friends, and big issues like hunger being only topics for world leaders. Like all the parents, my mom didn't give in to my definition of cool and I like all my friends were sent to school every morning annoyed by the early hours of the school. Amidst this I had my first encounter with the world of hunger. I was in the ninth grade and it started in the history class. History was my favourite subject. However I distinctly remember that it was one of those days when I was sitting more eagerly than I normally would be, almost with a tinge of anxiety, waiting for the lecture to begin. It was because that day we were to be shown a documentary. Well I know it was just a documentary but it was almost as if we were sitting in the theatre with popcorn ready to watch the next Avengers movie. It was our introduced as a part of holistic education to orient us with the happenings of World War 2.

The moment the teacher turned the projector on, it was however as if my heart stopped beating. The first picture I saw was that of a pile of dead bodies of Jews stacked on a carriage. I was taken aback almost trying to hold my tears. I could appreciate the ribs, the spine and even the face with only skeletons showing on each dead body with not even a little mass appreciable. I was so shocked that I couldn't even comprehend what followed. It was as if I had seen the face of death itself. All I remember is however what the teacher said in the end. She told us that amidst the world war, the struggle was not confined to the 2 nations confronting each other on a battle field. There was a simultaneous internal fight to live which was reflected in streets throughout the world where people could be seen contesting for food. Even on the days they were provided with food she said the quantity would be far less than what could satiate their hunger. Ultimately all this lead to millions of deaths.

I distinctly remember wondering wouldn't a death suffered by a gunshot or carbon monoxide in the gas chambers be much less painful. There was a sense of uneasiness that the thought "How hunger made people die a thousand deaths even before their heart actually stopped beating" brought with it. The apathy or powerlessness that I felt till that instant, somehow seemed to be fading away with a surge of anger arising from somewhere deep in my heart, thinking about how this state of life was still a reality and I did not care to bother. The documentary left me in tears and for the first time in my life I understood what the value of food was. That day, I decided not to waste any food that I was fortunate enough to get in my tiffin. This realisation was infused with a determination as a 14 -year old that I wasn't going to wait for some political initiative to do what needed to be done on my part.

My second encounter with hunger was around the same time when I saw "The Pianist"- a movie based on the Nazi Germany and I saw a man licking the food off the street because his hunger was way beyond comprehension. Sanitation and hygiene were questions that he could afford to address. I was disgusted but at the same time I was forced to question the plight of those who had to survive endless days without a single grain of food. I thought of countless refugees who had to flee from their homes in Syria, stood in refugee camps waiting for food in long queues and I felt a sense of uneasiness in my heart that how could we not care.

So, when I went to college a few years later and got the opportunity to join an organisation called Robin hood's army, a group of youth who would take initiative to take food being wasted at restaurants to those in need, I was all in. The tireless service of the people in the group who would take food to the poor at the end of the day made me feel things could after all become better and we could at last see a world without hunger. I felt a great power in my own life, welling forth from the spirit of youth, the determination not to give up. Through the passing time I saw the apathy and powerlessness in my heart turn into optimism. I was beginning to see how youth alone-together could change the situation.

After a certain amount of sensitisation to the idea of hunger however as years passed, I somehow saw myself standing again aloof to the realities of the world when again as a medical student I was introduced to the two horrifying diseases, kwashiorkor and marasmus. Two diseases that arose out of a deficit of food, seen in children mostly belonging to low socioeconomic backgrounds made me reflect further at the root of the problem. What struck me the most was that while these conditions governed the lives of so many children who were dying of hunger, simultaneously there was also a large fraction of the population facing the problems of obesity. I was forced to think what was the way to eliminate this evil of malnutrition, both under and over-nutrition, from the lives of people.

On further pondering over the question, I started to learn that hunger in this world is not only limited to certain sections of society at large but also exists as a part of the disparity. It flourishes within a household where there is uneven distribution of food amongst the children based on gender, where a boy being the pride of family was served better food than his sister because he has to work to get money to the family. This further forced me to contemplate whether just giving food to the people in need would solve the situation. It didn't seem that simple. The problem's origin didn't seem to lie in people's belly anymore; it was a matter of the hungry spirit lurking in the mind. It made people forget that each life was very precious, alienating themselves from the core spirit of sustainable development goals, of not leaving anyone behind.

"If my son gets good nutrition, he will get money for the house, daughter has to get married and leave anyway." "Jews deserve to die of hunger, their life is not worth spending on, especially at the time of war. "The more I thought about it, the clearer it became. It was no longer the hunger; it wasn't even about the political scenario of the country. It was about the disrespect for the dignity of life that we all have developed in our hearts with the passage of time. The idea that someone is not good enough because they belong to a certain caste, creed, colour or gender. That someone's life is more precious than the others.

The solution became clearer to me every passing moment. The remedy was right where we stood, not in a fancy parliament far from home. Actually, it wasn't in the next block or even a meter away, it was right there beating inside me. It was my own heart. My heart needed to learn to respect every individual, not leaving anyone behind, viewing everyone as a human first and their individual selves later. That moment of realization told me that my life needed no one outside to eradicate hunger.

We often feel someone out there rules the existence of life because it's convenient, isn't it, to not take responsibility to change the world. But what if each person decides to take responsibility for himself. Wouldn't the world automatically change.

Cesar Chavez once said "The fight is never about grapes or lettuce. It's always about people."

LEARNING POINTS

1. Respect every life not discriminating between anyone

2. Save food while you can by not wasting food in our tiffins or plates

3. Eliminate apathy and powerlessness from our lives

GOOD HEALTH AND WELL BEING

Health is wealth

Without it body is life in death

Only clung by the string of breath

Or you will be playing in a pile of wreath

*"Without health, life is not life; it is only a state of languor
and suffering- an image of death."*

– Buddha

Health, it's not a simple maths equation. Not saying that maths is easy but it is a subject where one plus one will always equate to two. However, in health there are no definite rules. It has countless variables of exercise, state of mind, environment, diseases and in today's time it has expanded its territory to an undiscovered terrain called coronavirus. So why are we even discussing an agenda which comprises diseases with so many variables and which in some cases doesn't even have a cure. We are here pondering over this agenda because of the infinite impact it has on us. We are talking about this sustainable development goal because in short health is not just something that impacts you but also your social and economic endeavours.

Amidst corona outbreak this goal may seem like a mockery with its action plans directly talking about eradication of communicable diseases. At the same moments, it seems easier to imagine a world without malaria or tuberculosis but tackling this global pandemic wrecking the world, is a problem beyond comprehension it seems. But we humans are not born quitters, so let's discuss this issue of health keeping the lives of our parents, siblings, partner or children in mind.

If even that doesn't convince you to embrace the third sustainable development goal, I have an anecdote to motivate you to think about this goal.

I remember one day talking to a helper in the college elevator. After the friendly courtesies and smiles we began talking. I was working to apply for a UNESCO program at that time and was working on finding an answer to the question "What is the biggest challenge according to me that the world faces today?" which was to be answered as a part of the selection process. I thought that it would be nice to understand her view about the same. The compassionate lady said that she thought a lot of people suffered from illnesses which caused a lot of suffering. These innumerable diseases that society has according to her was the biggest problem that the world had. She also said that only a healthy mind and body could truly contribute to society. I was surprised with her thought process given her education but having made good friends with her over the years I knew she always had a kind heart. Her insight really shook me. That moment was enough to make me understand that to eradicate misery from the face of the earth it was important to control the avoidable diseases prevailing in the world. So, this bigger picture amalgamated with an understanding of the potential that human life has, could be another motivation to start thinking about health in general.

As a child I would wonder, why do some people with cancer survive while others die. Even with the same type and stage of cancer, some live a very fulfilling and lasting life while some don't. I would often go to my grandma with this question, who being a very pious lady would say it was the way of God. If you do bad deeds you will have to live with the consequences. But this thought made me ponder why do the doctors give patients medicines at all. If they would have had to survive, they would even lead good lives without medicines if they had made good deeds. Things didn't seem to add up. Gradually when I grew up, I started viewing vaccines and medicines as the means to end people's problems because giving the power of determining our future to the past didn't make sense to me.

One day in the hospital while I was on duty many years later, I was taking the case of a patient ailing with colon cancer. There was a small, benign tumour which the doctors, if removed could enable the patient to live a healthy life. However, he said that his life was not worth the treatment and decided that he preferred smoking a few more cigarettes and drinking liquor to his heart's content rather than spend money on his medicines. Despite repeated attempts by the doctor to explain how the government would bear the expenses for the treatment the man was not ready to believe that his life could become any better. He left the hospital without allowing anyone to help him.

Meanwhile another man of approximately the same age, with similar complaints came to the hospital and was diagnosed with a similar form of colon cancer. Again, the doctor on duty explained to the patient how treatment would help him. This lad however was optimistic. He was ready to give it a shot. He understood the value of his life. He said with a smile to the doctor after every session of chemotherapy how the illness made him realise that having life in itself was joy. This not only gave the doctors the belief that the treatment would work but also encouraged the other patients around him to see their disease as an opportunity to see the beauty of life. The belief that the lad had in the power of his body to heal, along with his concern for others lives too, made all the difference. Soon everyone saw improvement in this young lad till he was finally discharged in a healthy state.

This incident made me go back to what my grandma said and I realised, didn't the person who decided to get the treatment make a good deed even in the present moment by deciding to take responsibility for his past. He once said "I live as a cause and not as a result." He decided to look beyond his past and through the present was busy paving the way for the future instead. That instance made me realise the value of present. Someone once explained to me how we feel happiness or sadness in a moment, the present moment. The present moment is thus all we have and if we decide to take responsibility for this instant, we can decide how our life turns out to be which is true even for our health. It's only a matter of how happy I decide to be in the present, how much I decide to care for my body in the present. It starts from appreciating that my health is very significant to the people around me and to the everyday value that my life creates. The question we need to ask ourselves is that how do I want to utilize this moment?

In a lecture that I was hearing about the coronavirus pandemic recently I was brought to the understanding that the power of the disease to win over your life is inversely proportional to the belief we have in our life. Yes, the solution to a pandemic maybe a vaccine but that too works on the basis of immunity. If your immunity is weak no vaccine can work, but if your immunity is strong there will be times when no vaccine is required. The source of this immunity however is our life force which wells forth from the conviction that my life is powerful which acts as the first line management to prevent any disease.

The minute in short we start understanding the value of our lives, we will start taking action to keep ourselves in good shape, start exercising a little more, eating junk a little less and start appreciating that we are the masters of our well being, in that very moment we are in sync with the highest form of well-being that exists.

"A healthy start comes from the inside." As said by Robert Urich.

LEARNING POINTS

1. Think about your family when you don't feel like working out.

2. Take care of your physical and mental health at this moment.

3. Immunity is manifested in our life condition.

4. If you decide to live a healthy life, you can.

5. Eat healthy

6. Exercise 5 minutes extra than yesterday

CHOICE IN DAILY ACTIONS

QUALITY EDUCATION

The opened book

The new look

That's how the world shook

Giving a new direction to the brook.

"When the day arrives, that education is based on a sense of purpose, all the lies and miseries of the society will be brought to an end."

– Tsunesaburo Makiguchi

Education is word that we have heard this word probably a zillion times by our parents, our teachers and our friends. Every person who comes and talks to the students has a view about this so-called education. Someone to academic excellence, someone relates it to the subjects that help you find a job and earn a decent living while yet someone else calls it knowledge. Also, as we grow up its description changes. In the earliest classes it was learning the alphabet and numbers alongside getting trained how to eat food without spilling. Later with time it became learning a set of algebraic equations to score good marks and moulding ourselves to behave in a way that is socially acceptable.

Mr Barack Obama in a recent speech that he addressed to the graduating class of 2020 said "All those adults that you used to think were in charge and knew what they were doing...It turns out they don't have all the answers. A lot of them are not even asking the right questions." This my friends, to open the young minds to asking the right questions is the purpose of education.

When I was a kid, a teacher told me after I fared badly in a test that I was one of ten children in the world fortunate enough to get the opportunity to study. I grasped the thought and felt perplexed by the idea of why those other nine could not go to school. Was it that they didn't want to or was it because they didn't have the resources? Some days in my childish mind, I would think I don't feel like studying. Let just one of them get the opportunity instead of me. But being a sincere student, I would again put myself to work with the thought that I'll create a world where anyone who wants to study, can.

I have been privileged to be taught by teachers who believed in me and helped me heal spiritually after I lost my father when I was 8, who encouraged me to see and understand the world in my own unique way, who forced me to think for myself by opening an unmarked map and making me search for hours together how the map was to be studied and yet others who taught me how to read in between the lines to understand what was not written.

I was grateful to all of them but still didn't understand what lessons beyond books had they taught me till I got an opportunity to teach myself. Out of the blue the help in my house brought his two children to the city. They had studied from a government school and now my mother decided she wanted them to get a better education. So, it was decided that they should prepare for an entrance exam for getting admitted to a good private school. Another decision was made that since I was good in studies, I would teach both of them. Summer vacations were on and I loved to boss the two around initially. I would take two chalks and the blackboard, lay down a pretty mat for us three and started my lessons. But it was getting harder by the day when they would not be able to comprehend what I was trying to teach. I continued the same monotonous routine till one day I realised they were trying very hard but though the curriculum was the same for both the old and new schools they were lagging far behind. What struck me the most was when one day the younger of the two pointed at a brick, red in colour and called it white. They knew the names of colours but didn't understand what they signified. I felt a sense of uneasiness when I thought about what I saw. I thought it was like when Helen Keller couldn't relate the word water to the flowing element in her hand. They, I felt, were blinded despite the perfectly able bodies They were disabled to communicate in spite of possessing the ability to use the pen which great men claimed to be mightier than the power of sword. I was forced to question our education system. From the next day on, I started making genuine effort to teach the two, not just what was in the text but really look at the world that existed beyond. It turned out they were bright minds waiting to be unlocked to limitless possibilities of life. I would read newspaper with them so that they knew what was happening in the world, showed them photos to illustrate that words gave them the power to express what they saw and voice their opinions, helped them read novels and some days would sit with them and simply ask what their aspirations in life were or if there was some problem that they were facing at school. I wanted to motivate them to dream big and reach for the stars.

I learnt that education was not just about scores. It was about teaching someone how to create an open mind and giving a child the key to unlock his own potential and think for himself.

Years later the older of the two who got into the private school, wrote a letter thanking me for believing in him and he has turned out to be a good hardworking boy who would wake up at five in the morning to study while he would make time to help his father with the household chores.

In my college years I saw my friends join an organisation called Make a Difference, teaching orphans in a nearby village. Encouraged by the heart of the organisation to make children a part of the society I applied to volunteer. In my interview I was asked why I wanted to help children. Since I had experienced the importance of education by the two kids from my childhood, I understood how a single child has the power to shape the future not just of his family but also of the society at large. So, my answer was a simple one liner. I said because I believe that they can turn out to be the next prime minister of the country. When I started to reach out to these children every time, I would see a spark in their eyes. They were ready to learn and grow. Their harsh realities made them understand how education was the only way out. I understood yet again the immense potential of each life.

Michele Obama the former first lady of the United States often talks of how education made a path for her to move forward from a life of what seemed to be with closed doors as a black woman, in the suburbs of Chicago, to one with infinite possibilities. In her book she talks about an incident where, once as a second grader, she was in a class where being from a poor neighbourhood lead them to get poor quality of education. The US system of community service became a strong driving force to better the education system of the school, when a community volunteer in the school addressed how each child deserves quality education.

Reading this I realised how it is truly important to sensitise the society not just to the idea of learning but education and not just for our own children but especially for those deprived of the leverage. How many of us question what kind of education is provided in the government school in our neighbourhood? Are the children even learning something or are the teachers even coming to take classes?

"The traveller climbed the steep slope, carrying a backpack climbing the summit, enjoying the view."

Education and that too quality education is the eyes with which the traveller learns to enjoy the view and sees the path to climb to the top. It won't make the hardships stop coming, nor will it make the slope less steep but it will help you press on.

We can solve the problems of our ministers not being educated, the teachers being incompetent, the poverty being eliminated from earth by a very efficient education system which has to be created by people in the community.

I have truly understood that the true purpose of education is converting knowledge into wisdom, something that only happens with courage and compassion for those who are not related to us. This is the most essential difference between a scholar and a bureaucrat or a politician and a leader. It is the most important ingredient in asking the right question.

LEARNING POINTS

1. Ask yourself the purpose of your studies
2. Study for the other nine kids who can not
3. Convert knowledge into wisdom with courage and compassion
4. Read books and watch documentaries to create an open mind
5. Consciously create open mind to ask the right questions
6. Fellow human beings teach us the most important lessons in life, so always have gratitude towards the human race

Gender Equality

Every life, defining the show

As the river of times changes flow

Well that's how the truth glows

Only when equality grows

"It is time that we all see gender as a spectrum instead of two sets of opposing ideals."

– Emma Watson

The term equality has a Latin origin. It can be explained by the '=' sign equating two sides of the calculation. One may then propose that it ultimately means men = women suffices the purpose of this discussion?

To explain, that I have an example. We can equate the value one in infinite ways, into what could be countless values all ultimately meaning the same.....that is the value one.

For example, $5-4 = 100-99 = 3-2 = 7-6\ldots\ldots\ldots = 1$.

Thus, equality doesn't mean being biologically the same or having similar talents. It means being different but still being a human before being a son or a daughter, a gay or a lesbian. It is a spectrum beyond just ideals of gender but a concept that resonates with the idea to incorporate the fact that human life is the ultimate value of 1. It is the string that binds us together. Thus, it's not about how we are different, it's about how we are alike. How we all are composed of 70% water, some flesh and a soul.

The fifth sustainable development goal gender equality is something I can personally relate to. It is not just about how the men need to change but how there is a need to empower everyone equally. I was born into a family where my father wanted a son. At the age of 8 when my father passed away, leaving behind a family with my mother, and her two daughters I began seeing that it was not just him. People would pass comments about my mother's vulnerabilities and some days I could sense the fear in her voice when she would tell us to be conscious of who we talked to. I was curious to learn why my mother was gripped by the fear.

I gradually observed how people would often come to the house to pay their respects for the deceased. I have personally never been a fan of the idea of giving condolences. People rather than giving hope make the person feel more helpless of the situation and pretend to understand the pain when they can't. It's better to care genuinely and give hope to the person I believe at such time rather than pity the person's situation.

Anyways, these so-called relatives would go on for hours about how the situation was tough with two daughters to take care of. They would tell my mother, "There is no son to support you. A son can take on anything, these daughters even if smart are an added responsibility." Even despite our mother never letting us feel any inferior I understood that if I were a boy, I would be considered strong. Subconsciously it started playing with my head. I stopped playing with my dolls, started wearing loose clothes, stopped applying henna and started trying to fit among the boys by making efforts to learn how to play football and cricket. I became the "tomboy" but was annoyed when I still was somehow seen as an inferior because of my gender.

I wasn't allowed to play cricket and was often told to play games that girls play. I was forced to feel I will never be good enough just because of my gender. This is something, that almost every woman faces in her life. I went on to play nationals in table tennis and still was not allowed to practice with the boys who thought they were superior to me just because I was a girl. This was unfair. And to top it off, despite all this life still had the audacity to have situations where not once but many times I was cat called or touched inappropriately.

But ironically over the years I had even learnt to suppress my feelings because I learnt that the norm of society says that boys don't cry. I wondered if it wasn't a satire in itself that we wanted to be treated like boys but when a boy would cry, I myself would label him as a girl. What kind of a mind had we developed with time that while fighting to be strong as a gender we ourselves had declared the gender weak. We had learnt to label a good friend as a bro, we had learnt that we had to behave in a particular way not to lead a guy on. Very subtly we had let discrimination creep in within our own minds unknowingly.

With passing years, I started seeing the flaw in the system. I wanted to find a solution to this problem not just for the side called females but for the large spectrum of people who faced such problems. I wanted an all-inclusive way out. I seeked the panacea to this evil by observing the women around me more carefully. I saw my mother who despite all the winds of life was always smiling, never complaining how hard the situation was. She managed to raise her two daughters to be an engineer and a doctor while she also worked her way through a business which was in debt to become a lady who everyone looked with respect and awe. She was a woman, a mother, a daughter but no one dared to mock her. Another life that touched me was that of a caring mother, a wife and a gynaecologist by profession who smilingly took care of her kids many a times making their favourite delicacies while continuing to contribute to the society as a doctor.

These women made me realise that first you need to love yourself, the way you are because till you don't believe in yourself no one ever will. It means when you are powerful within irrespective of the body you are given your charisma will command respect. Looking at them I felt it's okay to cry, it's okay to feel, it's okay to be a woman but what is important is to feel strong from within despite what life throws at you. I realised that happiness lies in accepting oneself. And when that would happen no one would dare question your strength. Second, they taught me that feelings and logic seen with the bigger picture in mind go hand in hand. If you have compassion to help people then your logic will create ways to achieve it transforming the world, little by little. When knowledge in one's mind is combined with the courage and compassion in one's heart it leads to wisdom which transforms the society. So irrespective of our gender or our emotional needs if we decide to think about the greater good, we can create a better world for ourselves and others. Third, they taught me how to smilingly fight this battle towards equality because what finishes hatred is not hatred but kindness. Phyllis Diller once said "A smile is a curve that sets everything straight."

Men who see women inferiorly do it out of their insecurity which originates from the lack of respect for their own life. They feel the need to suppress women to feel stronger and more powerful. We as women feel angry, sad, frustrated and myriad other emotions everyday which I understand but I am still not a feminist. Why? Because I'm an equalist who understands that to uplift the status of women in the society you need to first empower the men to believe that their life is powerful enough to not be affected by any strong woman. Equality won't come till, we are okay with a boy crying, playing with dolls or dancing a classical dance form and being himself in whatever way that is most convenient to him. We need to start by letting person be comfortable by allowing them to show who they actually are deep inside without feeling judged. Equality won't happen with anger that men are not worth being addressed as humans. It will come from the respect towards dignity of life be it a man, a woman or a transgender. It will come when the entire spectrum of mankind is seen as a human first.

So let us paint the mural of our identity as a human without any hesitation. Let's learn from others but not envy them. Let's be who we want to be. Let others be who they chose to be because this life is way too valuable to waste trying to be someone else or to pull others down. This life is meant to fly high in the skies of equality and humanism. It surely requires courage to start this revolution in our own lives, to respect those who have seen us inferiorly and above all to respect our own lives . But precisely because we have the courage to question the norms of society, let's start this journey within. Ultimately, we are made of the same water, flesh and soul.

LEARNING POINTS

1. Love yourself the way you are

2. Respect others for who they chose to be

3. Walk with a smile in the face of hardships

4. Heart + Mind = value (if for the bigger good)

5. Let's not judge anyone

6. Gender is a spectrum, not two poles of a magnet

KNOWLEDGE + COMPASSION + COURAGE = WISDOM

CLEAN WATER AND SANITATION

Inside out

That is how change is brought about

Cleansing the negativity bout

And the environment will purify without a doubt

"More people have mobile phone than have a toilet"

– United Nations

Sanitation is a major issue that plagues the world today. More people die of diseases due to bad sanitation than due to in war itself. It's a sad set of affairs how something so controllable is leading to people losing their families. According to the statistics given by the United Nations 1.8 billion people in the world are consuming water contaminated with faecal matter. About 2.4 billion people lack access to basic sanitation of toilets. Around 40% of the world faces acute water crisis. These alarming figures may not be affecting us directly but if nothing is done to make amends, we will soon collide paths with the menace that is caused by the situation.

Having been brought up in what is called city beautiful, Chandigarh, a small town in India which acts as the capital of 2 states I have been brought up amidst clean roads, greens all around, chirping birds, meticulous planning of the city and my favourite the beautiful Sukhna lake. The city is clean and a paradise on earth. It was the first planned city of independent India designed by a French architect, Le Corbusier who designed the city in the shape of a human body. The capitol complex forms the brain of the city, the green patch of land the lungs, the commercial centre the heart and the housing areas the limbs. I hadn't seen much littering around because citizens were aware about sanitation due to high education standards. It was the first city in India without any slums and citizens all over the town often voice their concern about the cleanliness of the city. However, I got my share of exposure to the poor sanitation infrastructure of the country when in summer vacations I visited my cousins in Delhi. Delhi was a contrast with narrow streets, high pollution, plastic bags and packed food items littered all around the city. The holy Yamuna river banks were the worst as they were stuffed with garbage, well, heaps of garbage and the foul odour engulfing the air would be too much to bear. It would always disgust me how people were surviving in that area. It seemed like they had no respect for the water that many animals and birds drank in order to quench their thirst.

Citizens in Chandigarh understood that if they left the city and its water contaminated the people around them would suffer and so their respect for life helped the create clean and green conditions of living. Caring for the sanitation of city thus became a symbol of showing respect and gratitude towards fellow civilians. The schools too actively took part in this endeavour and would encourage children to go beyond their books to understand the importance of sanitation and clean water by putting dust bins in every corridor of the school building. Initiatives were also taken to make us students clean the school premises so that we could discern the bad effects of littering around.

Since I had learnt early in life the importance of sanitation so when the Swachh Bharat Abhiyan initiative (Clean India Drive initiative) was taken by the Government of India it was nothing new to me. Along with my sister, I had for years been the proud advocator of 'no throwing wrappers out of the moving vehicle movement' and 'no wasting water while brushing or bathing movement'. We felt an overwhelming sense of victory when we saw that it the movements that started and ended in families like ours had created a difference around because the next time we went to Delhi we saw the size of the heaps which had risen to form hills of garbage over the time were finally reducing.

I realised the importance of this goal further in my college life. I was living a comfortable life away from the problems of sanitation when last year despite being in the coastal city of Mangalore, which receives heavy rainfall there was an acute water shortage. The rain hardly took place despite the monsoon months arriving. My hostel did not have enough water and we were told to store and utilize water for 3-4 days at a stretch which seemed like almost an impossible task for the 500 inhabitants. The issue extended throughout the city. Residents were supplied with limited tanks of water by the government. To arrange for basic drinking water became a struggle let alone to have the liberty of getting water to wash clothes. What till that point had existed only as a horror in our books was now our life.

Learning that how no toilets in the rural areas lead to more urinary tract infections in women and sometimes even leads death made me really reflect at the gravity of the situation. I realized that the crisis was much nearer than we had expected and that the solution had to be found in an all-inclusive manner.

Gradually I understood that this sustainable development goal needs an integrated approach to be dealt with. I read through a case study based on an initiative taken in the town of Arcata on the northern coast of California. Collaborating with scientists from Humboldt State University the local community took the initiative to create waste water treatment system within the natural ecology by creating a sanctuary with biodiversity of fish, animals and birds amidst the marshes with flowers, algae and microorganisms to neutralize, absorb and assimilate the pollutants. A citizen's group called friends of the Arcata marsh protected the ecosystem and kept the wonderful project going.

The government of Kerala, (a state in India) along with the local people have taken initiatives to build toilets and has arranged sanitation drives to spread awareness about ill-effects of unhealthy personal habits like defecation in the open, improper disposal of human excreta, improper waste management and so on.

Such endeavours have youth working at their core. The youth who want to create a better world and have the courage to work for it have laid the foundation stones towards better sanitation and hygiene with their creativity, dynamism and energy.

Dr. APJ Abdul Kalam, the former president of India was an exceptional scientist. He underwent major challenges in his life. At a young age, he had to support his family by selling newspapers to contribute to the finances. He scored average grades in school and further failed to reach his dream of becoming a fighter pilot when he placed ninth in the exam and only the top eight were offered the training. However, he did not give up on his dreams and worked towards contributing to his country in different ways. He was a part of the first rocket launch team in India which because of no jeeps at that time was actually carried on a cycle to the place of launch. This spirit that he had to make his country feel proud and further facilitate well-being of the society was reflected in his speech, My Vision for India, which he was addressing to students. In the speech he said "You say that our government is inefficient. You say that our laws are too old. You say that the municipality does not pick up the garbage. You say that the phones don't work, the railways are a joke, the airline is the worst in the world, and mails never reach their destination. You say that our country has been fed to the dogs and is in absolute pits. You say, say and say. What do you do about it?"

Reading about him I understood that we all have problems in our lives. Some illness, some are battling financial difficulties, some relationship issues and yet others don't even know if they would be fortunate to have the next meal on the table. However, people who have the courage to dream, not just for themselves but others too are strong.

Let us use our education to create dignity, to be the change we want to see rather than to judge the person in front of us and look down on somebody. It is very easy to complain and point fingers but it is difficult to take responsibility. If we see something is not right rather than complaining things will never improve let's use the energy to create the change. We have the power, the creativity but nothing will happen till we have the courage to take the responsibility of a better world. Let us use our education in innovative ways to not leaving anyone behind because after all there is no better world for you or a better world for me within its own right, there is only a co-dependent world that truly thrives.

LEARNING POINTS

1. Let's start in with our own initiatives, something like no throwing waste out of the car movement within our families

2. Let us take responsibility

3. Let's stop complaining and use energy instead for action

4. Creativity + knowledge = change

5. Let's integrate within the society to create ways to find all-inclusive answers

6. Let's initiate the change

Affordable and Clean Energy

The radiating rays of the sun

The limbs of windmill run

Illuminating the world with some fun

Showing the 21st century, that's how it's done

"Our universe is a sea of energy- free, clean energy. It is out there waiting for us to set sail upon it."

– Robert Adams

Energy can't be created or destroyed. It can be converted from one form to the other only. Haven't we all studied this in our science textbooks? It is something that probably is etched in our minds as apple is to alphabet A despite so many words actually starting from the letter. I would often wonder that how does it matter if we use clean sources of energy as wind or solar energy and that generated from petroleum if it could transfer form. My friends often called me the energy powerhouse and I would also think in my horrible attempt to humour myself that could this energy be used to charge the dead battery of my alarm clock.

The importance of alternative sources of energy was a question that further appeared in our environmental studies tests that followed. Like any other child of my age I would write dramatically, "What matters my friends is the air we breathe has less carbon, less allergens and that we find resources which won't deplete. It's not just about one aspect of life on earth, it incorporates sustainability of life, climate and health all into one", only to realize it was all true.

Just as Dennis Kucinich a former US politician said "It's time for a sustainable energy policy which puts consumers, the environment, human health and peace first." With time I started to question how my switching on the AC, begging my parents to drop me off to the school in a car instead of taking the bus and not switching off lights was a part of this seemingly important question.

Theoretically I started understanding the need to have clean energy sources when as a 10-year old, in my geography class I learnt that petroleum was limited in the world and took millions of years to form again. I thought that with the amount of electricity and cars that we use, it was sure that coal and petroleum would get exhausted sooner than later. I started trying to understand what were the alternatives we had because I was scared that soon we would have no electricity. I was horrified with the idea of taking baths with cold water in winter months without the geyser working.

My elder sister was very creative. Around this time, she started working on a school project on the functioning of solar panels as a renewable source of energy. The idea was new to me and I was very excited to see how it would work. It was the early 2000's and the idea of making solar energy working models at that time was a relatively new one in India. It shocked the wits out of me when one day she kept the battery outside to charge and that night her model was more than just buildings and roads made of wood. It also had light. I was finally happy as to me I had found an end to the world's energy problems. A medium by which there will be no pollution and lots of energy. Wow! My sister was suddenly a genius in my eyes. I asked her "What made you take on this project?". She replied "People need a little sustainable light within and without". They were powerful words that perplexed me then but still seemed important enough to remember. Meanwhile our school was so impressed by my sister's model that over the years they decided to put solar panels up in the campus. Also, my mother thought it was a good idea to set up a few panels at our home and in the real estate projects she had undertaken as a businesswoman. Often people ask what can a child do to create a difference. I saw the difference right there. Often people ask what is the purpose of making a school project. I saw value right there.

Jane Goodall said empowering words "You cannot get through a single day without having an impact on the world around you. What you do makes a difference, and you have to decide what kind of a difference you want to make." While her fellow batch mates were busy cribbing about the project or busy working easy way out by using thermocol plastic to come up with assignment, I saw my sister through her efforts making a big difference. It was only possible because she was aware of what kind of a difference she wanted to make.

I next questioned the relevance of renewable energy when I understood that the electricity in our house didn't come only from the solar panels that were made in the house or from petroleum-based power supply which could be easily exhausted. It came from a dam in my state called Bhakra Nangal Dam. I figured out that the single dam provided electricity to almost all the inhabitants of 5 states in India. I was proud to look at how India was using better means to create energy but didn't seem to like the idea of how many people were displaced from their homes to create the dam. Later on, I studied about a similar project being undertaken over the river Narmada which had been facing protests. These projects soon turned into a powerful movement called Narmada Bachao Andolan (save the river Narmada campaign). I was further distressed thinking that if the people only were suffering and had no homes of what use would the energy be. It was a matter of people's happiness and security wasn't it.

My third confrontation with the subject of renewable energy happened when I had the opportunity to travel to Europe in summer vacations back in school and I saw giant windmills. They were fan-like gigantic structures which literally were thousands in number stretched over a large piece of land. By this time I was seriously speculating that how change could be brought about. I was determined to find ways to not let anyone suffer but also create sustainable sources of energy.

With many countries in the world pledging towards switching to cleaner sources of energy I wondered what difference would such promises make, if we continue to have dam projects and displace people. They did not have heart like my sister who wanted to help the world with her little project and that's when it struck me that it was all a matter of heart. That's what my sister meant when she said light without won't come till there is light within.

The heart to help people, to create a better world for the future generations, to create a world where no one is left behind. Courage and compassion, it is said, are two sides of the same coin. Only when a heart of compassion is manifested from within can we find the courage to take action for it.

This intention would only manifest when we respect every life equally, understanding the potential of each person, the capability each individual has to create a difference. When we understand that there could be a 15-year old girl in the village where the dam was being built who had the heart of building solar panels in the village, to create a better future and the energy to make a difference like my sister would we would not have thought of displacing her.

The moment our heart changes to respect for dignity of life our actions will create the medium to create a world illuminated with light.

After all, as a 13th century Buddhist scholar, Nicherin Daishonin said "heart is the most important."

LEARNING POINTS

1. There are endless opportunities to create renewable sources of energy waiting to be explored, let's explore!

2. It's time for a sustainable energy policy which puts consumers, the environment, human health and peace into perspective

3. Let us reduce our carbon footprint in small everyday actions of switching off light while walking out of the room, walking to cover short distances instead of using vehicles, etc

4. Let us use every project or research as means to make a difference

5. Let us create a positive impact on the world everyday

6. Let us create sustainable light within and without

7. It is the heart of compassion that is the most important

Economic Growth and Decent Work

A job that makes me leap with joy
And makes me feel more than a toy
The country grows as a result, Oh boy!
That is what truly makes me Roy

*"The ultimate resource in economic development is people. It is people,
not capital or raw materials that develop an economy."*

– Peter Drucker

In Japanese, the term economics is represented by a four-character Chinese expression which means "to bring order to society and ease the suffering of the people." The actual essence of the word thus, is in ordinary people enabling prosperity of their society and world at large through their occupation. Economy over a time however, has been aligned to prioritize a single individual's interest and security leading the rest too suffer. Obviously, the purpose of the economy is inclusive of a stable flow of money and resources within families. But the question is that will a stable economic condition at individual level lead to a sustainable economy for future generations. Mahatma Gandhi once wrote to a dear friend "Recall the face of the poorest and the weakest man whom you may have seen, and ask yourself if the step you contemplate is going to be of any use to him." Isn't that in the truest sense the true spirit of the economy. Only when everyone in the world ensures a stable economy by helping others do the same, is when economic well being can truly last.

A friend of mine is doing economic honours in a reputed university and was sharing her journey with me. She said that just studying the subject would not suffice. Getting good marks and securing a good job in a top firm was not why she wanted to pursue her interest in economics. She really wanted to contribute to the economy of the nation as a whole by working on the real challenge at hand by creating economic growth by reaching out to individuals who need help. Despite being a part of endless clubs and committees in college with a huge pile of college work and entrance exams to cope up with, she took out time to work towards this.

She, unlike the other people of her age, always had a unique style to create a practical effect. She started working on a project to create better working conditions for people in a village by trying to create jobs. She put her energy towards finding ways to manage waste and simultaneously create jobs in the same project facilitating sustainable development of the society. She with her fellow batchmates brainstormed on ways to design such a project that brought together the worlds of development and sustainability. They faced limitations in terms of shortage of resources in the community, and ultimately thought it would be wiser to start with the city itself since they produced more waste and villages look upto urban setups to initiate such projects. She and her friends started going around the city trying to understand first, what conditions of people from low socioeconomic backgrounds limited them from living a decent life?

They met a worker who for years had been going to an apartment complex in the city to collect waste and was working for a shrewd contractor. The waste in the apartments was disposed off by a shoot system. All the garbage would pass through the pipe and collect in a tiny semi open room. The people in the building did not bother to know the time slot of the worker to collect the garbage. As a result, lot of times he ended up bleeding due to waste gushing down through the pipe which a lot of times had pieces of glass that would directly come on to his head. Despite his efforts to communicate his condition neither the contractor nor the people in the building bothered to understand his plight and he was barely able to earn a meagre of $26 a month. More than one day he would end up home stinking zould not afford to eat food so that his children could have meals.

Seeing his working conditions my friend and her team felt the need to change the working condition of the worker. They took the initiative to create decent work and living for the worker so that he could live a dignified life. After running errands and they along with their faculty came up with ways to support the worker, by creating a system for him where he could sell the waste directly to a factory. All the profit that was generated was now his to enjoy and he now made a decent living by earning a minimum of $130 monthly for his work. Inspired by how this initiative had led to social and economic growth in that person's life, they took a keen interest to pursue eradicating the open shoot system all together. In a small attempt to help the worker further they put a bag at the end of the shoot system so that he no longer had to be in a situation where he would have garbage spilled on him through the pipe of the shoot system.

Another endeavour they undertook was to employ two women to segregate waste such that one would sell the biodegradable waste to a nearby nursery where it was used as manure and the other would sell the non-biodegradable waste like plastic to a factory so that it could be recycled. It resulted in both earning around $ 195 per month. This way yet again not only were they able to generate economic growth but also facilitate a better working conditions.

From merely being able to exist the three workers were now thriving all thanks to dedication of these students to make a difference.

Economy as a whole can be thought in terms of short-term progress or long-term progress. If we think of individual growth and see economics isolated from others it will not last. For example, if an employer of a manufacturing unit thinks of enjoying all the profits without rewarding his employees for their efforts sooner than later their interest in their work will start to diminish and the production will drop, leading to his own decline. However, if we want a long-term development of the economy we need to focus with solidarity towards a collective future. Re-humanisation of the economy is thus the only solution towards this endeavour.

In the current coronavirus pandemic, the doctors in India were forced to go on strike due to violent attacks they faced. They silently worked with black batches to show their indignation towards how people with corona have been spitting on their faces, stoning them and sometimes even throwing punches at them. If such situations continue obviously the young doctors in the country will be frightened of the situation and despite economic stability that a doctor enjoys, they will not be willing to give their best. I am not saying that the doctor is always right but is a doctor who after years of studying and now trying to treat patients, putting himself and his entire family at risk of getting the disease worth being disregarded. Or as a matter of fact is any human life worth such treatment. Even if the doctor is earning well, is such a working condition close to one endowed with the right to decent work and creating any value?

Yet again I question would economic stability in itself mean anything if the dignity of life is not maintained in the process.

We have always heard since we were kids that you earn respect but now, I have learnt that to earn respect we first need to learn the art of respecting the one in front of us. We need to truly appreciate that the way to develop economic growth and especially during such times is by upholding the respect of dignity of life. Only by doing this can we change the situation for the better. This was exactly what Japan did after World War 2.

Mr. Antonio de Gueterre the UN general secretary said in his speech once that to establish human rights socially, politically, economically and culturally was not just the goal but also the path.

LEARNING POINTS

1. People make the economy, not the resources or raw material

2. Economy is to bring order to the society and relieve suffering of people

3. Economy can't be seen in isolation, if the aim is to sustain it through generations

4. The respect for dignity of life lies at the heart of economic growth

5. Upholding human rights is the path to economic development of a nation

6. Economics is not just in our books, it is in our communities

RE-HUMANIZING SOCIETY
THROUGH PURPOSE

INDUSTRY, INFRASTRUCTURE AND INNOVATION

The burning creativity,

The power in purpose finding unanimity,

The endeavours and efforts leading to productivity,

That's how the world finds longevity.

"There's a way to do it better- FIND IT."

– Thomas A. Edison

Mariana Mazzucato, is a leading economist. She is the economic adviser to Scottish and South African governments and is currently a member of the United Nations Committee for developmental policy. She once said "If we look at Germany's infrastructure policy, it has been driven by its mission-oriented focus on green infrastructure. This affects both innovation and infrastructure, old industries and new. The German steel industry for example, has adapted to the policy by lowering its material contents through a 'repurpose, reuse and recycle strategy." German industries lead the world in terms of technology and infrastructure along with innovation. The secret behind this growth lies in the mission-oriented focus which though not convenient is a necessity in the current times.

When I was young, my sister and I would love to sit down on the floor in the heat of summer, in every summer vacation without switching the fan on and would construct buildings with the deck of cards. We continued doing this for hours oblivious to how warm it would become till our mother would come and show concern that we would die of heat stroke. We could do it for hours at a stretch and not get bored. My sister who now is a structural engineer fondly recalls those days as the ones which taught her the art of building innovatively. She, who is now working in her specialised field of earthquake resistant structures, would always say that the purpose of the building is to ensure people's safety. This sense of purpose was what led her into creating value in her industry.

Whenever we paid a visit to our mother's factory, we saw that many people worked there. Some people worked with full dedication, while others were lazy. But seeing the workforce in there always made me feel that it must be doing well. However, mom one day told us how the company was working in loss. My father had started the company by taking huge loans from the banks and after his death my mother was forced to take care of the business after having been a housewife for 16 years. Apparently, the industry was called the white elephant which was basically a metaphor to represent that just as a white elephant eats whatever you give it, similarly all the money invested in the market would always stay there and bear no profits. Moreover, the competition from Chinese goods and the innumerable factories that were opening in the country posed a great threat to the company which was focused on quality rather than profits. I, as a young child, was confused as to how a huge factory with so many people and machines and most importantly a hardworking employer was not doing well. Matters became worse to the point that there was a machine lying redundant in the factory and no one was ready to buy it even at a throwaway price. But the research and development team did not give up. Some years later the company innovatively started the production of biodegradable bags which were used instead of polythene bags from the same unwanted machine. The company was not only able to recover from huge loans but also won an award, by the economic times group for the sustainable work it was doing. That incident made me realise that any industry worked well when the minds of the people working there are put to good use to innovate beyond what was in their comfort zone.

Another venture that my mom took was to make artificial leather to protect the animals from suffering harm and she named the leather Vegetable leather. She would often say that this leather would save so many lives. When she would take me with her to exhibitions, I would often see people tie the skins of buffaloes, cows and snakes to their stalls and boast about it proudly. There were times I felt thoroughly disgusted by how these educated people didn't realize the gravity of their actions and I couldn't help but feel proud of what my mother's innovative mind had managed to achieve.

Getting inspired by her I started enjoying my best out of waste activities back at school. The next year during Diwali I made a lamp from used plastic cups and Diwali lights. I reused the same lamp for some 7 odd years to decorate the house. I also made paper weights with stones and painted them as my favourite cartoon characters. I started to search for means and ways to create my own little industry, through the infrastructure available at home and used my creative mind to create something new. I believed that if my mom could do it, so could I.

Through various articles and ted talks I was exposed to the minds of people like Arunachalam Muruganantham. He is a social entrepreneur who though hardly educated and belonging to a very humble background had created ways to start a campaign across India. He made a low-cost sanitary pad making machine and faced a lot of opposition in his village for the taboo associated with menstruation however he continued with his endeavour. Years later when he was finally able to make the machine, he decided against getting it patent under his name, even though that would have earned him millions of dollars. His heart since the start had been to uplift the living conditions of the women of his village. He started this endeavour when he heard that women in his village used dirty cloth during their period, which led to life threatening infections. So rather than earning huge profits for himself, he made women run small industries throughout the country. This not only supported women who could not afford to buy the sanitary pads but also gave thousands of women across the country jobs and a sense of better standing in the society.

The life of Dr. Verghese Kurien, the mastermind behind making India the largest milk producer in the world by playing the Architect in India's White Revolution too revolutionizes our outlook towards this goal. He empowered Indian farmers through formation of a cooperative called Amul where any farmer be it a male or a female, rich or poor would be allowed to pool their share of milk and 70–80% of the money paid by the consumers would go as cash to dairy farmers. They themselves created a dairy industry where the farmers would control the marketing, the procurement and the processing of milk and milk products as the dairy's owners, while hiring professionals for their skills and inducting technology, in managing it. A key invention at Amul, the world's first, was the production of milk powder from the abundant buffalo-milk, instead of the conventional cow-milk, short in supply in India. Today Amul is the leading company in India for dairy products and is providing thousands of people in India financial security.

This sustainable development goal in the truest sense is like the oil fuelling the other goals like economic growth, gender equality, no hunger and poverty, sanitation and many others. Without the belief that an idea can be transformed into reality is a waste of our innovative brilliance. Only when we believe in the power of our dreams can we make them a reality. Obviously, we will fail in the process of innovation, but not trying for the fear of failure equates to failure itself.

Let's just think it this way, if you don't run in a race scared of the failure, how will you ever find out whether you were about to win or lose.

Also, once someone asked me when I was a kid, "Do you have big dreams?"

I said "Yes"

He said "Do you think there will be huge obstacles to make them a reality, obstacles as big as the universe?"

I said "Yes."

He said "Do you know someone who can make your dreams a reality despite those huge obstacles?"

I said "Yes of course, if they are my dreams, I can make them come true."

He said "So remember your life is bigger than the universe itself."

And he left with a smile across his face knowing his words had hit the right spot.

LEARNING POINTS

1. Mission oriented focus is the best way to innovate

2. Repurpose, reuse and recycle

3. Nothing is a waste if you innovate beyond your comfort zone

4. It is not just limited to huge industries, it starts from our home industry

5. More than education it is our determination to create that helps create infrastructure

6. Don't let the fear of failure stop you from trying

7. Don't give up at the last moment, you are almost there!

8. The power to change the world and win over hurdles lies within you

REDUCING INEQUALITIES

Equality for equals

Seems like there are no sequels

Is opportunity a prequel

Let's create the world that is co-equal

"When everybody is somebody, then no one's anybody."

– W.S. Gilbert

Charles Darwin, the most prominent figure in the world of scientific evolution gave the theory of survival of the fittest. It is a concept that has played a subtle role in the minds of millions across the globe and is not limited to the perspective of evolution but also to the way society functions. Based on our stance on the limited understanding of the theory, over the time, we have questioned the complete eradication of inequality placing ourselves in a convenient position not to take responsibility to make amends. However, I propose a social concept today called equal opportunities versus equal status. Fittest takes into account several factors, starting from social, physical, psychological, genetic, cultural and many more which are themselves variable based on the opportunity provided to a person in the course of his life. The aim here is to provide equal opportunity. For example, every child gets an opportunity for a good quality education. Obviously, every child won't become Einstein but at least they have the resources to become one. Also, they will get the opportunity to be the best versions of themselves.

I loved being a kid. Back in my nursery days, I would never agree to come home directly after school. My best friend was a year senior to me and lived near my grandparents' house. Every day I would go to his house after school. Everyday my grandmother and mother would have to convince me to come home but I, being in my full element, would be stubborn but alas, ultimately had to give in and go home. The reason that I loved those days which one mostly doesn't remember anything much of was the bonds of friendship. I think kindergarten is a place where one makes the best friends because everyone is so pure that they love you and respect you irrespective of the fact that you are the naughty kid who doesn't stop talking or the introvert who keeps to himself. Everyone at the end of the day would play together and feel respected, without any judgements of society affecting them.

There is one thing that happens when we start growing up- we start understanding the world. And based on what little understanding we have we start judging those around us. In the book 'Heidi' through the character of the grandfather the author Johanna Spyri tries to throw light on this development in the human realm. Ironically, we all are unique, however being different is still not acceptable. Oh! That child doesn't score well, stay away from her; that person doesn't have any friends, he must not be a good friend.

In my case it was- she doesn't have a father, she is not normal. So, every day I would sit alone in the lunch break, eating my food feeling as if I didn't belong with the other kids. They did not know what life meant to me and did not know what to say to me. So, it was just easier to avoid. There were days when me going and trying to talk to others was considered as a desperate attempt to fit in, which maybe it was but I ended up being a laughing stock. I called this emotion as the refugee feeling, the sentiment of not belonging because I co-related it to what those poor children in the warzones who had to leave their homes must feel when they went to a new society and tried to fit in. And I was not the only one. I realized that those of us who did not fit in, were different. I sometimes even thought maybe I was an alien trying to be a part of a world where I didn't belong.

One day I was very frustrated with what was going on in the school. It had been 5 years with me being left out of almost every conversation going around in the school without me complaining even once. But that day I could hold on no more and I went to my mother and said that I couldn't go to school anymore and burst into tears. My mom was taken aback but patiently tried to understand what I was going through. She was however never someone who would give sympathy.

She in her stern but loving way said "You are like the sun, bright and radiant. There will be clouds to hide you but continue shining."

Those words gave me the power to believe in myself. Next day on, I started cheerfully greeting everyone in the class first letting go of my own judgements about them. I learnt first that to feel equal I needed to feel that even they had the capacity to love me the way I was. I too had judged them on my limited experience in life and had to first initiate the change within. Also, I was no longer afraid to be called names because I was who I was, the bright sun, not ready to stop shining because of the clouds that tried to stop me. By the end of that academic session I was friends with almost the entire batch and everyone started loving me. I was no longer the refugee.

Having been in that space of being judged I had decided to never let anyone go through what I had suffered and made a point to talk to everyone in the class. A friend of mine wrote to me on the last day of school saying "I shall always remember you as a person who can love the whole world and still have space in her heart" something that left a great impression on my mind making me feel I had made a difference.

Mr. Barack Obama once told a group of women that "Do you settle for the world as it is, or do we work for the world as it should be?"

I had decided in those trying years that I wasn't going to wait for someone to come and make changes for my life to be better. If they were my problems my life had the solution to them.

I was greatly inspired by people like Nelson Mandela, Rosa Parks, Martin Luther King, Abraham Lincoln and many others who had dealt with various struggles to create a world with equal opportunity for all. Nelson Mandela was in prison for 27 years an act of cruelty and injustice done to him in the name of colour over the years. In prison however, he had seen the hospitality of a white guard towards him and had realised that a person is not defined by his colour but by his heart. He saw the potential in every person irrespective of their caste, creed or colour to respect the dignity of life through that guard. When he was released from the prison he said "As I walked out of the door towards the gate that would lead to my freedom, I knew if I didn't leave my bitterness and hatred behind, I'd still be in the prison." He was not the person who fought for the rights of only his kind but also of those who had been the reason he couldn't meet his children for 27 years. And how was he able to bridge the gap between black and white in the society we may ask, it was by bridging the gap in his own heart by making a conscious effort every moment of his life.

Reducing inequalities is a goal that doesn't exist outside our lives; it lives deep within us. It lies when we feel "that person is good for nothing", "I'm weak", "things will never change" because we have made judgements way early without thinking that the person in front of me is a life, same as mine.

It is only by bridging inequalities in our hearts that this goal can be made into a reality. This process however finds its roots in us understanding that our differences are our strength, not our weakness. I would like to quote the lyrics of a song from the hindi movie Swadesh, based on the concept of reducing inequalities,

Tumne dekhi hai dhanak toh	If you've seen a rainbow
Bolo rang kitne hai	Tell me how many colours are there
Saat rang kehne ko	There are seven colours to speak of
Phir bhi sang kitne hai	But they're so closely associated
Samjho sabse pehle toh	First understand this
Rang hote akele toh	If these colours were separate
Indradhanush banta hi nahi	A rainbow would have never formed
Ek na hum ho paye toh	If we don't manage to unite
Anyay se ladne ko	To fight against the injustice
Hogi koi janta hi nahi	There won't be any people
Phir na kehna nirbal hai kyun haara	Then don't say why did the weak lose

Let's remember we are here to make rainbows, together.

LEARNING POINTS

1. Equality of opportunity is the goal

2. Let us all become the best versions of ourselves

3. Let us make friends without prejudices

4. Shine bright like the sun with hope even if there are clouds to hide you

5. Let's not settle for the world as it is. Let us create the world as it should be

6. Let us not be prisoners of hatred

7. Let us focus on creating rainbows by fighting against injustice

8. Let us not let anyone suffer what we have endured

9. Let us eradicate the refugee feeling

SUSTAINABLE CITIES AND COMMUNITIES

I walked through the street

The one where dignity and respect meet

Living the life of sustainability on repeat

Till the dawn of hope rose to great

*"What is the use of a house if you don't have a decent
planet to put it on."*

– Henry David Thoreau

According to United Nations "The aim of this goal is to make cities inclusive, safe, resilient and sustainable." We may wonder why only cities and urban areas. According to statistics about half the world population lives in cities which is sure to increase in coming years. Cities in current times are becoming more and more unsafe with crime rates in places like Chicago and Delhi skyrocketing, finding their roots in poverty and hunger that engulf the masses. The inequalities in cities like Mumbai are rising with one part of the city overflowing with sky-scrapers while the other half overcrowded with the biggest slums in the world. More than 828 million people in the world live in slums and the value seems to be ever increasing. To top it all the pollution in cities and massive energy consumption are further causes of great concern.

Sustainable as a word has evolved for me over a period of time. Initially it was a set of random alphabets put together that I had to memorise. I didn't like the word much as I would often lose marks in the dictation tests because of it. Later my equation with the word changed as it became a long word in social sciences which could fetch me marks. With time I understood it means something that was maintained at a certain level or rate, so in college it became the definition of our life that existed between the college building and the local bar till one day we stumbled across the word in our community medicine class where the heading of the chapter itself was sustainable development goals and now it meant something new all-together.

While writing an article for a college magazine on sustainable development a few months back, I started thinking what sustainability means in a college campus set up. It means a good education system where every teacher imparts knowledge not just with PowerPoint presentations but their practical experience. Where each student learns from the teacher's expertise on the subject and then applies the knowledge gained to his or her profession and community with a sense of purpose. Where there is good transportation arranged for the students so that no one feels the need to buy a vehicle, thus lessening the carbon footprint on mother earth simultaneously decreasing the financial stress of the students. Where hostel food may not yummy but is nutritious with greens and is made under proper sanitation precautions of kitchen so that the students can have the energy to work to the best of their ability. Where the hostel security is strong enough so that the students can play around freely in their leisure hours, so that their body and mind is fit. Where administrative systems in college are strong enough to take action to ensure the safety of girl inmates of the hostel and so that no one is cat called and touched inappropriately in and around the campus. Where the college administration is approachable, the library access is available to all and everyone gets equal opportunities to stand for the council positions. When all this happens, and the students start reaching out in the community to apply the knowledge to create a better society with economic growth and better living conditions for everyone a sustainable setup is created. This practical use of knowledge itself is wisdom. When such a sustainable ecosystem is established at college level, a sustainable city and further a sustainable nation is formed. This in itself is creating an environment of everlasting growth for the students, the institute, the community, the environment and the nation.

This all however rests solely on one aspect- how much effort is everyone ready to put in their jobs. Starting from the administration to the students, from the guards to the help in the hostel if everyone starts doing their job well sustainability will no longer be a dream.

It's always easier said however than done. It's easy to question the system. What's difficult is to check our own actions. To question that am I doing my best.

In my college there have been incidences of people from other colleges often coming and creating ruckus in front of the girls' hostel. They would cat call the girls and touch them inappropriately. The matter became worse when the girls asked the guards to help and they said it was not a part of their job. This led to frustration developing among the girls who when shared their concerns with the lady in charge, got to hear that they belonging to a particular gender should be careful. For years I saw the girls bear with what was happening, cribbing that guards don't do their job properly and complaining that the restrictions were over the top. However, no one ever tried reaching the administration about it directly. Finally, when I reached the authorities, they took action to create better conditions to facilitate safety. The point that I want to make here is just hoping for a sustainable world won't suffice. We need to fight for justice, that's how change happens. It's also about giving our best rather than just expecting others to change.

South India in the business world is seen as a great market with opportunity for growth. So, I started observing the coastal city of Mangalore where my college is to understand what made southern part of India special.

Mangalore, though a small coastal town in the state of Karnataka but has a high literacy rate. The public transport in the city from the local buses to the ferry are all affordable and extremely efficient. The roads are clean and the city is well kept. The medical infrastructure of the city is well developed as proven by the fact that more than 99% of the deliveries in the city take place in the hospitals. The Anganwadi in the city (centres run by the government to teach children and provide them nutrition while also reaching out to the community to create awareness about health) is one of the best in the country. The public library access is available for anyone who wants to study. The education standards of the city are good and there are many non-governmental organisations in the city that work extensively towards projects like cleaning the beach, preventing food from getting wasted, reaching out to children to teach them and are mostly initiated by the huge student population in the city. There still are problems in the city but the respect for dignity of life in the small religious town in India makes it an example of a sustainable city in my eyes.

In the movie Shawshank Redemption, the life of prisoners in the Shawshank prison considerably improves when one prisoner starts working towards creating a sustainable atmosphere. He opens a library, introduces a system for prisoners to take exams so that they could achieve a diploma and also teaches a fellow inmate how to read and write thus creating value. He was able to do that because he believed that there was still hope left in the life of convicts.

Natalya Sats was the mother of the children's arts movement in Russia and served as the president of Moscow Musical Theatre for Children. She too was wrongly convicted in her youth due to politically driven motives. However during her life in prison, she transformed the jail into school and theatre. The idea struck her when saw the talents in the fellow prisoners. Rather than feeling self-pity or feeling regretful about her situation she used the adversity as an opportunity to create growth. She put her mind to creating a sustainable society by initiating a value creating endeavour in the prison cells. She truly embodies the spirit of the person who walked up the steep slope with a heavy backpack, up to the peak of the summit, enjoying the view.

Learning from these great individuals' lives, I understood Dr. Daisaku Ikeda, a Japanese philosopher's words

" A great human revolution in just a single individual will help achieve a change in the destiny of a nation and, further, can even enable a change in the destiny of all humankind."

A sustainable city or a community is thus formed only when we first create a sustainable self who understands the limitless potential of life and rather than becoming complacent see every obstacle as an opportunity for growth.

It's all a matter of becoming the change I want to see.

LEARNING POINTS

1. The reaches of this goal extend and permeate the change to the other goals

2. Obstacles are opportunities for growth

3. Stop complaining, start acting

4. Don't waste time on self-pity

5. A great revolution in your life will change the world

6. Don't miss the opportunity to make a difference, and you will see the power within you

BEYOND I,
ME AND MYSELF

RESPONSIBLE CONSUMPTION AND PRODUCTION

The new toy is the best

I want it without the rest

But the package of pollution comes as a guest

For that's what is life's jest

"Every time you spend money, you're casting a vote for the kind of world you want."

– Anna Lappe

According to a research done, we would need 5 earths to support the world population if the entire humankind started living like people in America. With more people in the world progressively shifting into the category of middle class the consumption and production of goods has increased considerably leading to excessive rise in the stress that is put on mother nature.

Aren't we mostly responsible in our actions, especially, in buying the best Gucci bags in the whole town and then keeping them safely. Then why bother about this sustainable development goal. Because my friends this goal goes beyond the bags or belts that we all are obsessed about. It extends to the fact that at this rate the world by 2050 will need 3 earths to sustain the demands of people, not just in our luxurious lifestyles but also with respect to the food we eat. The solution lies in 3 words- reduce, reuse and recycle.

Till certain point we have all thought these to be limited to the pages of the 3 R's in the environmental studies books which had nothing to do with our everyday lives. How to practically use these 3 R's in our everyday life thus is a crucial prerequisite to achieving this goal.

Michelle Sohn, a brand and business strategist defined an ethical consumer as "An ethical consumer looks for products which above all, are both friendly to the environment and also to the people who produce them. They are aware of the consequences of the production, consumption and disposal. They have clear expectations of how they expect a company to behave and expect ethical companies to have ethical standards."

I was acquainted to the art of recycling when I would be passed on my sister's clothes which I wouldn't mind much because they fit me decently well. Even a new school bag would be bought with the condition that we would use it for a minimum of 3 years and so we had to keep it in good condition. My sister was the careful one and I had to struggle to keep the bag in one piece. With time I learnt to keep my school bags in good condition and used my last school bag for some 5 years. It was not a financial necessity, but it was our mother's way of teaching us practically that Earth has enough for everyone's needs but not enough for everyone's greed as said by Mahatma Gandhi.

My sister had the habit of collecting the extra pages of her notebooks at the end of every academic year and made new notebooks out of the unused paper. I carried on this legacy and built on it by also removing the cardboard from the previous notebooks and binding it to make it look as good as new.

My teachers also played a role in teaching me the art of reusing. By making us all students pool books and create our own library one taught us how not only to reuse but also share. Every week each one of us would issue a book and read. I actually completed my Harry Potter series that way without having had to buy them. Another teacher of mine would make us write notes by folding the paper into half because he said "we mostly never used the second half of the line anyways." This helped me in finishing the notes of the entire French revolution chapter of history in two pages, obviously considering the fact that I had painfully small handwriting.

In school when we studied about the rainwater harvesting system I was intrigued by the idea and told my mom that we should reuse rainwater. My mother, always a person of action, actually got the system created within the house in no time.

Diwali is the festival of lights when the entire country decorates their homes with flowers, lights and candles. Last year after festivities my college friends collected all the flowers from the entire hostel and dried the petals to make potpourri out of it. In small ways people in my environment have showed me responsible consumption and production of things.

During the lockdown my mother asked workers in her company as a strategy to keep their minds busy to find innovative ways facilitate the growth of factory post pandemic. Three days later, the workers in the factory came up with the idea of making mattresses for the hospitals from scrap. They were able to thus not only reduce the waste but also recycle the waste and reuse it for the benefit of the society amidst the pandemic.

Impressed by the work at my mom's factory I too started thinking how could we magnify this concept of consumption and production to the problem that the world faces at large. As a student and an ordinary citizen, I wanted to make a difference. In the meanwhile, one day I was watching a movie (which by now you probably would have figured out is my favourite pastime) that posed a satire on the education system. The movie was an adaptation of a Hollywood film Accepted and was renamed as F.A.L.T.U (useless).

The plot of the movie was based upon the premise that there are countless students who don't score well and because of that don't get admission to colleges. Also, with the Indian society laying emphasis on seeking admission into top courses the stress level is so high that children succumb to the pressure and face depression. These children, start feeling they are good for nothing; they are useless and don't have a purpose to exist in the world. However, when the same children are allowed to shine in their chosen fields they do wonders and live satisfying lives creating immense value in their communities in their own unique ways.

In the movie the person who inspires others to go behind their passion, the hero was a son of ragman. The ragman says to his son when he finds out that his son has created an illegal school to help children find purpose in life "You are even a bigger ragman than I am. You found ways to turn these useless rags, the students, into assets to the society." This gives the hero belief in his own power and he is able to get licensing for the school after a legal battle. This movie made me realize how this same concept of reduce, reuse and recycle could be used in life as well and every time we spark the hope in a person's life, we are able to make the person start afresh with a new resolve to win in life.

Reuse, reduce and recycle is only possible when you see the potential in something in not an obvious way. But we often forget to do that with people in our environment. Each one of us has visions and missions. Maybe in the current situations and circumstances a person may not be able to shine but each individual has a unique mission that is his or her alone. When each person starts believing in themselves and begins encouraging those around them to live up to their mission world would become a better place.

In the book The Alchemist, the Alchemist described gold being nothing but refined recycled lead from which impurities had been removed. We all are that lead trying to turn into gold but if we don't realise that the gold is within us, we will never be able to shine. And when that gold manifests from within our life we would be able to manifest the potential in everything that we come in contact with. Isn't that what alchemy is all about?

LEARNING POINTS

1. Our choices as consumers shape the future of production

2. Reduce, reuse, recycle

3. Buy products friendly to the environment and producer

4. Be aware of the consequences of production, consumption and disposal

5. Through sharing let us learn to reuse

6. Let us try to keep our things responsibly

7. Let us give hope to the people around us because their life too has a potential that has not been unlocked

8. Let us polish the mirrors of our life and remember even if we are just lead right now we can manifest the gold within and without

Climate Action

A world with birds and clear skies

Through the joy of construction passing by

A world anew will ahead us lie

Because the climate is the only thing that can help us fly

"Unless someone like you cares a whole awful lot, nothing is going to get better. It's not."

– Dr. Seuss

Climate is often confused with the idea of existing weather conditions. Weather is something that prevails for a short period of time while climate persists for decades. Weather change in this sense is not as big a problem as climate change because the latter affects many aspects of the society starting from agricultural practices that define the food on our plate to the multiple natural calamities that have engulfed our world. Furthermore, in the passing few years the change has been dramatic. As we see the ozone layer depleting, water level rising and biodiversity decreasing, we can't help but feel alarmed. What used to be summers has been replaced with killing heat-waves causing deaths in various countries. Summer vacations are no more about children playing in parks. Kids end up being at home throughout the holidays playing video games because of the extreme weather. Summer in tropics has been replaced by the desert heat and things don't seem to be getting any better.

I always seemed to love with nature and its bounties. The winds, the grass, the plants, the rain, the moon and the stars were all my friends. I enjoyed conversing with them and would merrily play around in the open skies. It was the best time of my day when every evening riding my bicycle, I could feel the gentle breeze across my face. So, it was natural that I took interest in environmental studies as a subject. In one of the lectures while we were studying about air pollution, to encourage all her students to reduce carbon footprint on earth the teacher came to school on a bicycle. It was something that made a huge impact on me. I started insisting on walking or using my bicycle to travel short distances. Her small act of putting into action what we studied made me realise environmental studies if only read in books will not create any value. It's about applying the knowledge in our everyday life.

Meanwhile I had a junior in school whose parents were reputed doctors in the tri-city area. Everyday her father would cycle with her to school as the family decided against buying any vehicle to prevent the environment from depleting further. Despite being in a space where they could easily afford any car they wanted, the commitment their family had towards a better world made me always look up to their family as an inspiration. They could have created thousands of excuses to avoid the exercise, by saying we have to treat a lot of patients and hence have no time or that it was too cumbersome. But their family continued this endeavour willingly, motivating many others in this process.

Soon enough inspired by the family I started taking part in the awareness creating program undertaken by students of various schools in tricity. Trying to make things innovative, once we danced around the lake on the Katy Perry song 'firework' by changing lyrics here and there to create awareness among people about the significance of climate change. We remember it vividly as being an embarrassing attempt but the fact that we at least had tried, made us feel rather important on this journey as stakeholders of a new age.

Meanwhile stories of people like Wangari Maathai, who took the initiative to plant millions of trees across Africa, to transform the world for better inspired me to love mother earth even more. She said "It's the little things that citizens do. That's what makes the difference. My little thing is to plant trees."

When I was around 6 years old, I used to like hearing Michael Jackson's song heal the world. I still remember once I was singing with a group of grown-ups, mostly my mother's friends. Everyone stopped singing the song midway when they saw me reciting the song with utmost passion. I as a 6-year-old was convinced that I will heal the world even if I was all alone, a spirit that stays alive in my heart. My fervour however gave the people around me the courage to believe that if a 6-year-old could believe she can heal the world, they surely could do something about it.

Mr. Barack Obama once said "We are the first generation to feel the effect of climate change. We are the last generation that can do something about it."

Things have been hard in 2020. We all have survived the horrors of a pandemic, wars, cyclones and plane crashes. However, amidst the pandemic there is a silver lining and that is the earth healing. Despite the fact that the various memes of how iron man told Thanos "the earth is closed today" may seem relevant today, I personally feel the earth has never been so open for animals or plants since we humans started taking over the planet. Finally, the air is cleansing, Ganges has dolphins playing around, animals including deer, horses, etc are on the road, there are reports of ozone layer taking its normal form and finally the air is a treat to breath. We humans over the years have thought we are super smart. We live a clean, happy life while dumping our waste outside our homes, where other organisms live not realising that even if we throw out waste into our environment it will come back to us in one way or the other. We want to rule the world because we think we have immense brain capacity but what we forget is that if we use 10% of our brain the dolphins use 20%. It's just that they have used it to co-exist with the flora and fauna in the water instead of destroying it.

Let alone the flora and fauna, the reckless behaviour of humans has caused umpteen disasters in recent past starting from earthquakes to famines, cyclones to the ongoing pandemic, which have become the source of human suffering. Like it is said the universe will always give back to us what we deserve. It's simply the law of cause and effect. You study for an exam, you score well. You don't study, you won't score well. Similarly, you take care of the environment, it will treat you well but if you don't, you will have to bear the wrath.

We humans are ignorant that stops us from living a happy life. The unawareness that even the animals and birds around us are lives. The unmindfulness that sometimes we in our own shells of jealousy which rise out of fear and insecurity ignore the vulnerable sections of society. Countless times we forget that even the mother earth can sustain everyone's need but not our greed.

There are a lot of people who criticize Greta Thunberg but her life is truly inspiring to me. How many of us have even tried to do what she is trying to do. It is easy to complain, it's difficult to act. At least she is trying to do the world some good. She is fighting a battle for people like you and me. Even despite us criticizing her she has not given up.

Courage and compassion, it is said, are the two sides of the same coin. If you have courage to think beyond yourself and take action towards that thought becoming reality, then the courage translates into compassion and vice versa. Neither can exist without the other.

Greta Thunberg said once "Sometimes we just simply have to find a way. The moment we decide to fulfil something, we can do anything. And I'm sure the moment we start behaving as if we were in an emergency, we can avoid climate and ecological catastrophe. Humans are very adaptable: we can still fix this. But the opportunity to do so will not last for long. We must start today. We have no more excuses and neither the luxury to delay it any further."

So, let's start today. Let's start now. To those who question how, start simply by treasuring the life in front of you, be it a flower, a fish or a fellow human being. Dig a little deeper within to find courage to be compassionate. Because compassion will expand your life to see beyond the scope of scholar into the realm of being a world leader in your own right. Once that happens action is not far away.

LEARNING POINTS

1. Convert words and knowledge into action

2. Be the change you want to see

3. Get out of your comfort zone

4. Create awareness

5. Do the little that you can by planting trees, using bicycles, etc

6. Be optimistic

7. Move out of ignorance and jealousy

8. Awaken the courage and compassion

9. Make the conscious decision to co-exist like the dolphins do

LIFE BELOW WATER

The moment flows by like a molten sapphire

Deep blue silences

No Earth below

No sky above

The rustling branches and leaves

Saying that only you are here

Only me

My breath

My heartbeat

Such depths like this

Such loneliness like this

And me only me

I now believe I exist

Zindagi na milegi dobara

We live on land and apart from the 70% of our body being made from water and the Adam's ale that we drink or take bath with, caring about water seems rather stupid. And the United Nations now wants us to think about life under water. Seriously! What's wrong with them? But where does the water we drink, the sea food that we so often relish, the countless herbal medicines, the biofuels come from? Does it not come from the vast expanse of oceans? And above all what if the water plants that provide oxygen start dying? Will we be able to live a happy existence?

It doesn't end here. The marine areas contribute to reducing pollution and help in waste removal while the coastal ecosystems prevent damage from the storms. Moreover, a well-protected coastal ecosystem reduces poverty by providing huge supply of catches and thus gets the economies of fisheries going. Another sustainable development goal that life under water supports is that of gender equality as most of the small-scale fisheries are run by women. Apart from all this seacoasts have always acted as a great source of tourism and recreation.

Sylvia Earle an American marine biologist and explorer in residence with National geographic said "No water, no life. No blue, no green."

Having been brought up in a landlocked state my encounter with water bodies used to happen when my father would take us on pilgrimage. We used to go to the holy town of Haridwar where the river Ganges exits the foothills of the mighty Himalayas. The river would be so deep for the younger me that my parents wouldn't let me go into the water. The only thing I was allowed to do was soak my feet in the refreshing water body. So, I got plenty of time to observe the surroundings. The place would be packed with people. I could see hundreds of saints doing some form of yoga or chanting their verses in their saffron dhotis. There would be mellow music playing around and bells ringing in the nearby temple. The water would be pleasantly cold and sometimes I could appreciate fishes swimming around. The energy was just ecstatic. Ganges is said to contain diverse organisms including small fish, Gangetic dolphins and a special species of bacteria that apparently cleanses its water thus making the river holy. But amidst this I saw something eerie. I didn't get that why people would keep throwing not just flowers and ashes of their ancestors into the water but also plastic waste. Wasn't the water too holy and sacred to do that. Even if it weren't holy did it not ultimately make the source of drinking water for countless Indians, I wondered. Later, I realised the problem was not just limited to the city of Haridwar. A lot of industries were built on the bank of the river across the northern plains of India to enable easy unaccountable disposal of waste. So, the river which was supposed to act as a source of life was now rather becoming a source of diseases.

My mother often says Hindi is a funny language. It has ways to always put the blame on the other person. In Hindi when we travel to Delhi we exclaim "Delhi nahi aya" (Delhi hasn't arrived yet) as if the city of Delhi had to walk and come to us. We don't like taking the responsibility that we are running late, and we are at fault.

Similarly, it's with our water. We externalise the issues of water and continue procrastinating, playing the blame game, the government doesn't do their job and the industries pollute the water. What can we do? Nothing will change with this attitude. What we need to do however is to start taking responsibility for our actions by not throwing another plastic item in water and by doing the bit we can. Robert Swan the first person to travel to both the poles, an environmental leader, a public speaker and an author said, "The greatest danger to our planet is the belief that someone else will save it."

Another key point towards finding a solution to this sustainable development goal is in undertaking innovative initiatives as youth. To cite a few examples, a few companies around the world have taken initiatives to use waste from water to create various items. A company based in Greensboro, North Carolina is using the waste from oceans to spin yarn that has been used to make over 2.2 million graduation gowns. Rather than further creating waste by using new fabric this company through sustainable fashion brought new life into the blues. Another company based in Hawaii is using waste to make soaps out of plastic. The company runs the entire project on wind energy thus creating a sustainable ecosystem. Big companies including Adidas and Parley have also invested in the cause and have come up with plastic sneakers. All these initiatives are just the tip of the iceberg many people will say.

Actual tip of the iceberg, my friends is the fact that not even 0.001% of the population is trying to do something about it except for crib and add to the pile of junk.

While studying for this particular goal I was really questioning what can I do to make a difference apart from making sure that the beaches in my neighbourhood are clean and creating awareness. But then while trying to see the bigger picture, I realised how these small acts of creating cleanliness in my environment were the crucial drops of the big ocean of change. Second as a student I recognised that we have the power to use our creative impulses to create something new. At least trying was something that I could do.

I realized that we allow ourselves to be swayed by the definition of failure as set by society and hence fearing the setbacks, don't even try. However, all these old people who define failure to us have failed in creating a world of no poverty, no hunger, better environment and in short, a truly sustainable world. Mr Barack Obama said in his speech the other day "With the challenge this country faces right now, nobody can tell you "no, you're too young to understand" or "this is how it's always been done." Because with so much uncertainty, with everything suddenly up for grabs, this is your generation's world to shape."

A lot of times students, including me, either end up living in the world of not caring about what is happening around them, involved only in their own personal and professional growth or are depressed and feel powerless that they can't make a difference. They either live in a superiority complex of being more important than their environment or inferiority complex of not having any value. However when we all start working as equals letting go of our insecurities which arise due to probably the massive competition in the world today and start seeing the bigger picture of a happy world overflowing with infinite potential we would be able to invent a world of our dreams. What we need to understand is that no mars mission happened with one man alone. It is only by moving together can we shape the world. The mars mission by India happened when a collective effort was made by a group of people to create something together by giving their best at each moment.

Despite various limitations like that of a minor budget that was even less than that of the movie interstellar.

It is all about the decision we make in the split second to break out of powerlessness and apathy. That moment, our life manifests the power to change the world even if the resources may be limited.

LEARNING POINTS

1. Let us create awareness of life under water

2. This goal will help in actualizing the other goals

3. No one else will change the world. It is a task for us to act upon.

4. Take innovative initiatives

5. Don't fear failure, because failure is not trying

6. Do your bit, because actual ocean is formed by small drops

7. Let us move together as equals breaking through our complexes

8. Where there is a will, there is a way

LIFE ON LAND

The nature's bounty on land

Making through mountain, plateau and sand

It is all about giving a hand

And every moment will be grand

"Nature always wears the colour of the spirit."

– Emerson

Life on land. Don't we very naturally relate this phrase to human beings? But to anyone who has ever owned a pet will know the other side of the story. It is an expression that includes the concepts of afforestation, preventing desertification and maintaining biodiversity on Earth. I never understood the phobia of animals that we humans possess, till I met my roommate. She is so scared of animals that even the thought of them being around (puppies included), can make her cry. This fear that is instilled in most of us city dwellers somewhere stops us from appreciating the beautiful spirit of life. Every life be it of birds, plants, animals or humans has great potential to love and the moment we understand this, we won't be scared anymore. Rather we will subconsciously start reciprocating what mother earth has given us.

When my father passed away my mother brought home a dog, the most enthusiastic dog in the world (well he should have been as he was my dog). He was a golden coloured retriever, whom I was petrified even to touch initially, but two days later he was my best friend. I named him Cabbie, something that was inspired from a movie. We would go on walks together, play hide and seek and would entertain ourselves with his yellow frisbee. I would play the mouth organ to which he would often add his melodious barks and whenever I put music on the recorder, we would end up dancing together. I would even celebrate raksha bandhan with him, a festival to celebrate the bond of siblings. It is a Hindu festival in which the sister ties a thread on the brother's wrist and prays for his long life while he vows to protect her. The problem was that the thread would stay intact only an hour or two on his wrist as he would chew away every fibre out of the thread. The times when I would be scared about something and would be crying, he would most affectionately listen to all my worries. In short, he was my best friend. Being with him for over 13 years I have learnt how wonderful dogs are and to the possibility of how amazing every creature in the world is.

Other non-human friends on land that I made included two doves who would often come for the grains that my mother loved to feed them. They would calmly pick one grain at a time and enjoy their evenings peacefully.

With this background when I studied about biodiversity in future classes it instantly became my favourite subject. I took on to the subject as fish loves water. While it was a nightmare for my friends to memorize all the names which were tongue twisters, it would be a treat to learn about the amazing flora and fauna that inhabits our planet. To appreciate the diversity that exists on our planet in depth, I would make trips to the botanical garden near our house and would stare at the various flowers for hours together. Those visits helped me understand Myron S. Kaufman's words "Watching something grow is good for morale. It helps us believe in life."

Another incident at helped me understand the ecosystem on land better. Parkash bhaiya, our house help, who was almost like an elder brother to me, loved innovating. He started working on a kitchen garden in our house some years back. Mostly we humans don't appreciate the fact that where our houses stand now, were essentially homes of various animals and forest land. So, when the vegetables would become ripe, a lot of monkeys would often come to treat themselves to the vegetables to bhaiya's utter dismay. It would be hilarious when a monkey would come inside the house holding a brinjal from the garden and eating it happily while bhaiya carrying a broom in his hand tried to chase the monkey away. Every time this happened I laughed the air out of my lungs. It made me see how the plants, animals and humans co-existed in my own little garden set up and I didn't mind sharing the vegetables with my fellow living creatures.

The rivet popper hypothesis used by Stanford ecologist Paul Ehrlich struck a cord with me. The theory equates the airplane to the ecosystem with the rivets holding it together, an equivalent to species. If every passenger according to the theory would start popping a rivet to take home with them causing species to become extinct it may not affect the flight initially but gradually with more rivets being removed the plane would ultimately collapse. Also, which rivet is removed is crucial, one of the wings, the key species of ecosystem versus those on the seats or windows inside the plane.

So, with this I began understanding the purpose of the ecosystem at large and the need for various wildlife sanctuaries, biodiversity parks throughout the world. But a question that used to spring up in my head was evolution has happened for ages with species eventually become extinct over the time. What was so different now?

While researching about the issue I read about how colonization of tropical Pacific islands by humans lead to extinction of more than 2000 species of native birds and how the Amazon rainforest called lungs of the planet were being chopped down to cultivate Soybeans or to convert the area to grasslands for raising the beef cattle. Even in my own environment I how there was a company trying to cut a patch of trees in my city which provided the supply of oxygen for almost the entire city and habitat for countless organisms.

Seeing all this I was angry at my indifference. I was furious that I directed my anger towards my friends for not listening while I myself had hardly not bothered about those countless organisms who had been shouting for years to stop the wreck that we had created. I was forced to help people in my city to support them in the movement they had initiated to stop the trees from being uprooted. I talked about the issue with anyone and everyone in my environment as a young kid to create awareness. Ultimately the court had to stay the project saying that the trees were much more important.

In this entire process I asked myself the question how many Cabbies' would be displaced in the process of cutting down trees just for a factory that gave us a new set of clothes which after wearing twice we won't even care about. The thought itself brought tears to my eyes. We have learnt our emotions, our anger, our pain, our misery, our happiness but we forget to understand that be it a dog, a cat, an earthworm, a fish or a tree they too have emotions. There is a reason after all why they respond to love.

According to a United Nations report on this goal they said 31% of the land that makes up the forests provides us humans with the majority of oxygen, water and food. 1.6 billion people in the world depend on the forest for their livelihood. About 75% of the world's poor population is affected by the land degradation that has been going on. Forests are home to 80% of the animal, plant, and insect population and because of our reckless behaviour 8% of the biodiversity has become extinct and another 22% are at high risk.

So, don't you think it's important to give life a pause occasionally and think, about the countless lives apart from us that exist and I'm not just talking about the 7.2 billion humans. Can't we think about how they feel the way we want others to think how we feel. Can't we for once think of them as lives too.

A.A. Milne the author of Winnie- the-Pooh once said beautifully "Just because an animal is large, it doesn't mean he doesn't want kindness; however big a tiger (Tigger) seems to be, remember that he wants as much kindness as Roo."

LEARNING POINTS

1. The closer we are to the nature the better are our spirits

2. Don't fear animals and other organisms, at least try to accept them

3. You can find the best friends in nature

4. Observing biodiversity helps us believe in our own lives

5. Let us be kind to animals, for we have displaced them

6. Let us create awareness in our life and that of others about the ecosystem

7. Let us pay gratitude to nature for its boundless gifts of oxygen, water and food

8. Let us be kind and think of other's emotions the way we would want our emotions to be thought about.

9. Let us act based on above points in our environment

OPTIMISM > REALITY

PEACE, JUSTICE AND STRONG INSTITUTES

The burning flame of justice within
With the truth taking its place, to begin
Its matter of creating hope by digging in
Through unity and trust finding dawn wherein

"Peace comes from within, don't seek it without."

– Buddha

Krishna Srinivas who served as the president of World Poetry Society, in his poem the five elements, under the elements fire wrote,

Eternity is here

In infinite now,

The illuminated now,

In freeze of fate

In death of hate.

Having been a fan of biographies since my high school years I was familiarised with the lives of children in Syria, the people in Israel and Palestine, the effects of war on young girls in Pakistan and the lives of people in Japan who had suffered the wrath of world war 2 in the worst possible way by the nuclear attacks. Through books, I developed the conviction deep within my life to end wars all together and would often tell my mother that I want to go to Syria to create peace.

I read about the life of former President of University of Philippines, Dr. Jose Abeuva, a few years back. Both his parents had been freedom fighters fighting against Japanese oppression in the country. He along with his 6 siblings were captured by the Japanese government, and his grandmother was killed. Ultimately both his parents too were brutally tortured and killed and left to the wild animals. Later when the country finally attained independence, Dr. Abeuva rather than bearing grudges against the Japanese, was determined to create peace. While he served as head of United Nations University for 8 years which had headquarters in Tokyo, he made an effort to establish peace and understanding between the two nations. He declared that "Throughout history there have been many leaders of war but there have been few leaders of peace. I am determined to help change this." His life truly moved me to develop compassion in my life for others, even if they are mean to me with a firm resolve to bring peace.

The interest in history that I had inherited from my parents further sensitized me over the years to the sufferings of people post wars. Once going through a book, I came across the works of peace scholar Elsie Boulding. An incident from the 1960s was narrated in the book. She was once attending a conference on disarmament and asked the participants who were specialists in the field, how they envisioned a totally disarmed world would function. However, to her surprise, they said that they did not know, nor did they bother to know as their job was merely to describe how disarmament is possible. Dr. Boulding thought to herself how can we create the world whose vision has not been created yet.

This question made me think that as a youth, I am trying to create a new age, a new world without giving a thought to what kind of a world I want. So began a journey that my thoughts undertook to address the ringing question in my head "What kind of world do I want?"

I started by thinking of a world without war, well that seemed extremely important. I, however, wasn't fully convinced that just wars were the cause of suffering. Gradually I thought that people fight amongst themselves even if the country is not at war. Also, around this time the corona pandemic broke out and I strongly felt that the answer must include the health issues. After giving more and more thought to the issue I came to realize that only a world with respect for dignity of life will bring actual peace. The origin of war ultimately is from people's heart and the ailments that people suffer from is because they don't care for our own health.

To further explain the words of Buddha and how peace starts nowhere outside but from within, I have a narrative from my own life. My father was a great businessman, one of the first real-estate builders in the region. He had a loving family with a beautiful wife and 2 daughters and a decent house. But as his business grew, he started getting conceited. He took huge loans of millions of dollars from banks to establish an industry which he had no idea about, started an extra marital relationship with a woman, bought a gun to protect himself and began travelling in a bulletproof car. He wanted to believe he was bigger than everyone else in the world, something that rose from his insecurity that someone else was more capable than him with the competition in the market increasing. Japanese thinker Kiyoshi Miki said

"Jealousy arises out of insecurity." He must be at peace with how things were, almost everyone in his surroundings thought, till one day he shot himself with the same bullet in the same bulletproof car that he bought to protect himself. It was very similar to the plight of nuclear weapons which though initially created to establish peace, had turned into means of mass destruction. My father thought he had created external measures to ensure peace and security but what about the upheaval in his heart.

Obviously, the incident impacted me a lot. Not just as a daughter, but also as a fellow human being. I had to read about firearms in my forensic medicine classes a few years back and remember how I couldn't help but cry thinking what inner turmoil his life must have gone through. Forced to think about what had happened I understood was that hope was the only thing that could create peace. Hope was a battle we have within the depths of our own life to attain peace and security. Someone asked me recently what does hope do? I answered that hope is the thing that was given to young Charlie Chaplin by his mother when he said he didn't want to live. It was something that the almost deaf Beethoven created in his heart when he wanted to die because he wasn't able to compose music anymore. This four letter word thus became the source of origin to the glorious career of Charlie Chaplin and of the composition that is the epitome of peace "Ode to Joy".

Wangari Maathai said once "In the course of history, there comes a time when humanity is called to shift to a new level of consciousness. To reach a higher moral ground. A time when we have to shed our fear and give hope to each other. That time is now." The time to create hope is not far in the future, it is now and the place to create this is in the heart of the person right in front of you.

If someone is hungry what do we do? We make food and give them. But what will happen tomorrow when again he has no food? At some point the person needs to learn how to make food for himself. The important point is we teach the person how to cook food. Over the years I have thought many times what would have helped my father not commit suicide. I thought maybe me hugging him and telling him things would be okay would have sufficed but that would just be cooking the meal once, overcoming his angst momentarily. He needed to believe that he could get over it, that would have meant him learning to cook for himself. He went around telling the world that he was strong because deep inside he felt weak. It's like when after a breakup people tell themselves they don't need love because they don't want to be hurt again but deep down, they still want to feel the love. So, in short, hope is not telling someone things will be alright. It is telling them that they have the power to make things alright just the way they are.

Peace my friends comes, only when we are comfortable in our skin, okay to be who we are, not pretending to be someone superior or inferior, while remembering the power within. And when that happens, we are at peace with ourselves and others around us. And this peace that we find by acceptance of ourselves leads to fight for justice because it is not coated with insecurities. This network of hope and acceptance leads to justice and peace.

A Scottish poet, Robert Burns wrote

"Tyrants fall in every foe!

Liberty's in every blow"

LEARNING POINTS

1. The time to eliminate hate from our hearts is now

2. Let us create a vision of the kind of world we want to live in

3. Let us replace anger towards injustice with determination towards peace

4. Respect for the dignity of our life and that of others is the way to peace

5. Peace is created inside out beginning by accepting ourselves

6. Network of hope is more powerful and infectious than the corona pandemic

7. Let us remind each other of the power within

8. Obstacles are opportunities to change the world

Partnership for the Goals

Standing together, walking ahead
Not gripped with fear of any threat
We, the phoenixes, the youth, the revolutionaries as said
Launch into the new age like a powerful jet

"When spiders unite, they can tie down a lion."

– Ethiopian Proverb

I always tend to get fascinated by people. Where there are a group of homo-sapiens, there often exists one of the two ends of the spectrum. One end is unity while the other end is competition. Dissecting through concept of competition further, if it is seen from one end of the telescope, it opens one to opportunities to better oneself but from the other end it limits us from growing. Even within an organization working with people we may feel overwhelming at times with the incredulous diversity of individuals and their minds. For an introvert it may become a struggle to function amidst umpteen people but does that mean one should not try. My mother always told me that there are two types of people in the world. One that push you down to move up and the other who supports you to move along seeing the potential your life has. Yet the silver lining lies in how the first kind of people teach us to believe in ourselves. So, where there are human beings one can always find reasons to grow.

Over the years I've come across various kinds of people. Some are kind, some frustrated, some selfish, some jolly and there are also some whose sadness makes you question your own existence. Honestly, many a times I have been part of the conversations that how individuals can be backstabbers like Brutus that do rounds in the current times. However, like almost everyone despite having been at the receiving end of being taken advantage of, I have this quality of seeing good in everyone in the long run. This way even if myriad times I have felt betrayed, I have learnt to grow out of those situations. I have learnt to become a river that flows despite the stones, because I realised no one grows in comfort zone. So, for sure to deal with people can be torturous many a times but if they were not there in our lives wouldn't we have become complacent and lazy.

And if that still doesn't seem like a good enough reason to give a chance to humankind let's remember what Hellen Keller said, "Alone we can do so little together, together we can do so much." Which brings me to the other end of the spectrum and that is unity. I have had the opportunity to be a part of many organisations over the years. In my school there was a club called Sahodaya (Rising together) Club which used to organise evening classes and meals for children, visit old age homes and orphanages. We would sometimes go and play cricket with the children from orphanages and would make an effort to listen to the elders whose families had left them to the old age homes. I was a part of that club only for one year, but I always used to look forward to being a part of any activity undertaken by the club. Being a junior and that too a shy one, I wasn't a significant person in the club. Rather I was bullied to do a large part of the work while others took credit for the effort but still, I felt in my own little way that I contributed to society. Gradually with time I also learnt to stand up against the bullies in the club because I did not want to give up on helping the vulnerable sections of the society. So, it was a two-way win, I was able to help people and learnt to stand up against wrong that was happeneing.

Another campaign that I frequently indulged in was a part of Wada Na Do Abhiyan (Don't Break Your Promises National Campaign). I remember us going to what was like the Times square of my city to advocate for various endeavours like importance of voting, right to eco justice, etc. Once we made songs to create awareness about the pollution and yet another time, we danced our way into embarrassment to advocate for the voting rights. However, because of the act we were able to encourage around 100 people who had never voted before to vote. In our own ways we were making a difference because boldly we took creative actions. In the campaign a group of 5-6 children from various schools in the tricity area would come up with constructive ideas to raise awareness about various social issues. It included singing songs, doing plays, dancing, writing poems, etc to raise consciousness among the masses and the effort that everyone put in the endeavour was itself a testimony of how partnerships among people helps us create a better world.

My mother being the president of the rotary club in her area would often emphasise on the importance of partnerships by telling me how the rotary clubs throughout the world, along with the governments across nations created the foundation to help eradicate polio. So even when I would shy away from group activities I would participate in the small events thinking I was contributing to a better world. One of such initiatives included plantation drives that our school would initiate every year on Van Mahotsav which was an annual tree planting festival, celebrated in the month of July for an entire week. During this festival thousands of trees are planted all over India. Initially it was probably to impress my mother and my teachers though that I would volunteer, however gradually I understood the importance of conservation of trees and forests. So, by the time I became a senior in high school I would try to help with the heart that this was a festival celebrating the very spirit of life itself.

Even in my college life I have seen various non-governmental organisations doing work in their own unique way to help in the advancement of society. The Robin Hood Army, Make a Difference initiative and Voluntary Service Organisation were few organisations I closely observed. The students in these organisations in their own ways have helped the vulnerable sections of the society by working with their communities by helping eradicate hunger, giving quality education to orphans and cheering up children in the paediatric wards. The small efforts made by these organisations even if for an hour or two on Sunday mornings has helped many lives. Another organization very close to my heart is the Soka Gakkai International (Value Creating organisation) which I have been a part of since a very young age. It is a partnership of people to help uphold the dignity of life and to create a network of hope. Through an inner transformation in the depths of one's life, something called the human revolution, the people in the organisation help each other grow as individuals.

I was just talking to my college roommate who laughed when I said we are walking towards a better world, a new age. She said that the world can't improve with one person taking a thousand steps, she said it was to be the other way around. I countered however by saying that if I decided to better myself every day, every day I better the world. While writing this book I have realised we students and a large portion of youth think very little of ourselves. We feel we can't make a difference. It is the big companies and people with money and power that can change the world.

Let's however paint the picture of a world where each one of us starts creating value in our small actions which starts reflecting in the way society shapes up. For example even if one child doesn't die of hunger because of the work done by you as a member of Robin Hood Army, or one child you taught at Sahodaya club becomes a source of inspiration for others, or if one person less dies of polio because vaccine reached him on time.....you have made a difference. It's a matter of moving on from petty fights asking ourselves, how courageous am I to have compassion for people in this world I am not related to?

So it's not about flashy initiatives it's about how ready we are to get out of our comfort zones on a Sunday morning to teach a bunch of children unrelated to us, or how much effort we are ready to put in studying a little harder, or how much hard work and confidence I have in my research project not so that I get to top schools but so that I can make this world better is all that matters. Dreaming to get a top rank in an entrance exam is futile if it doesn't correspond with a dream to help transform the society and people in it.

So, the question at hand is "Is my heart just to move further in my career or is it something bigger like making a sustainable difference?"

LEARNING POINTS

1. Choose between unity and competition

2. Choose between pulling others down and walking ahead together

3. Choose between getting defeated by problems and using them as springboards to success

4. Choose between letting others teach you apathy and you teaching them kindness

5. Be part of partnerships, even though it may not comfortable but it will help you to grow

6. Check yourself, am I being selfish

7. See the bigger picture and use your energy to overthink important things rather than being dragged down by small obstacles

8. Create compassion in your heart to make a difference

9. Stop under-estimating your potential

Author's Note

I hope some of you have been able to reach this part of the book without losing your mind. Well the idea of writing this book is to understand the 17 sustainable development goals and realise that those goals don't exist outside our life. I as a youth have thought countless times "How can I make a difference?"

However, while writing this book I yet again reaffirmed my faith in my own life and that of others to make a difference. Definitely my patience, which by the way is not my strength, was tested beyond its limits of its being. But what I understood by the end made me feel powerful – It's all about *respecting the dignity of life*, believing that life in itself has limitless power to create good. I further understood that this practice could change the world. Not an easy task for sure! The struggle was to remind myself every moment – "Respect dignity of life, Inayat". Well I won't say that I was able to achieve this in every moment of life, but I know what I felt every time I did. It made me, a medical student, 'live for knowledge' realise, *knowledge only when combines with courage and compassion is wisdom*. So, this sense of *rehumanising my sense of purpose* in life helped me move out of apathy and powerlessness into *youthfulness* and hence, move towards sustainable understanding about the world. That realisation of the world was that 'change is the only reality and *optimism* the only way out'.

And this my friends, is why and how writing this book taught me

I > REALITY

www.ingramcontent.com/pod-product-compliance
Lightning Source LLC
Chambersburg PA
CBHW021445210526
45463CB00002B/638